A MOTIVATIONAL MINDSET FOR TEENS

PRACTICAL LESSONS AND ACTIVITIES TO IGNITE
YOUR INNER DRIVE, BUILD POSITIVE HABITS,
EMBRACE PASSIONS, AND START TO CONQUER GOALS
IN 31 DAYS

SYDNEY SHEPPARD

CONTENTS

INTRODUCTION

Imagine this: You're scrolling through social media, and post after post, you realize that everyone else is achieving incredible things—getting straight As on their report card, starting and excelling at a new hobby, or even starting their own business. Whether you've ever thought about achieving them or not is irrelevant. The point is that others are achieving great things—and you're not. "Why not me? Why can't I do these things?"

If this sounds familiar to you, you're not alone. We have all been there. It sounds cliché, but it's true. I'm not just saying this so that you can feel better. It always feels like everyone else is living the dream while we spend our time scrolling through Instagram, wishing it was us.

According to a survey by Ritter (2023), about 27% of teens feel overwhelmed about what the future holds. This could be due to various reasons, but finding the motivation to plan for tomorrow could make a big difference. Ken Poirot (n.d.) said it best: "Today is your opportunity to build the tomorrow you want."

As a teen, I know there are so many difficult situations that you may be facing at this point. It could be societal expectations to be perfect, social pressure to fit in with everyone else, or even academic pressure to do well in school so that you can do something with your life one day. In some cases, you might even be faced with difficult family dynamics and competing with other siblings to be successful in your parents' eyes and make them proud.

All of these factors can easily leave us overwhelmed, feeling lost and like there is no way we can live up to those expectations. People often try to combat this by telling us, "Just be yourself," "Stay positive," or "Hang in there, it gets better." When, Sydney? When does it get better? The truth is that it won't just get better, especially not overnight. We can do so much to make sure that it gets better sooner rather than later.

Whether you want to change your outlook on life, are feeling stuck in your current season, or desire personal growth to become the best version of yourself, I've got you covered. It's important to know what you would like to get from this book before you begin reading it to ensure that you benefit from it and have the ability to transform your current life situation. Take a moment to think about it and write it down on a piece of paper or your phone. Keep it close and refer back to it whenever the lines start to feel a little blurred. Knowing what you want to focus on will give you a greater chance of success.

I am passionate about helping teens and young adults reach their full potential by making small tweaks to their mindset. This book has been specifically written for you to reap the following benefits:

- Unlock your potential: This book offers over 32 activities and many exercises specifically designed to help teens and young adults recognize and harness unique strengths and talents. You'll learn how to dig deep and discover some strengths you might not even know you have.
- Master goal-setting: Learn how to set achievable goals and break them down into smaller tasks. By understanding the art of effective goal-setting, you'll be empowered to aim high and achieve whatever you put your mind to.
- Build resilience and confidence: Through practical advice and exercises, you'll learn how to bounce back from setbacks and build self-esteem to try again.
- Cultivate a positive mindset: With tips on how to think positively and practice gratitude, you'll find it easier to handle stress, deal with negativity, and maintain a happier outlook on life.
- Manage time effectively: Get insider techniques suitable for the busy lives of teens and young adults. Learn how to prioritize tasks, balance academic and personal pursuits, and avoid common time-wasters. We don't always need to make mistakes to learn from them. Sometimes, the best thing you can do is learn from others' mistakes.

- Become an inspiration to those around you: You will learn how to sustain your motivation and discover ways to inspire those around you. By becoming a source of inspiration for others, you enhance your journey of personal growth and reach a new level of feeling like you make a difference.

Gone are the days when everyone else's life looks better. The strategies included in this book have been carefully developed and considered to ensure you achieve the best possible outcome if applied correctly. You will learn how to motivate yourself to do better each day and live a more fulfilling life supported by success and happiness.

My daily job involves working with young adults to help them improve and shift their mindset where necessary. I started a *You Are Your Mindset* series to be able to share these tips and tricks with more people than just the ones I can personally reach. Three books have already been published in this series—this is the fourth one. The others deal with cultivating a growth mindset to become more resilient, how to develop the right money mindset, and encouraging a gratitude mindset daily. You can find the full titles of these books in the conclusion in case you want to check them out.

As you work through the pages, you will come across various activities to help you apply the theory shared in the chapter. Take your time to understand the concept and complete the activity before moving to the next section. You can take as long as you want to complete the activities. I would suggest buying a notebook or dedicating an electronic notepad to all the activities. You'll need it for most of them.

We start with what it means to have a motivational mindset and the difference it makes. Then, we will explore how to discover your inner drive and cultivate resilience and confidence. Next, we look at how you can nurture your passions and turn your dreams into achievable goals.

To achieve goals, it's important also to understand time management and build new habits to sustain motivation. Finally, we'll examine how you can use this newfound knowledge to inspire others. In the last chapter, I've included a 31-day challenge where you will complete an activity a day.

So, if you're ready to ignite your inner drive, build positive habits, and start conquering your goals, you're in the right place. It's time to turn the page and begin your journey to a more motivated, fulfilling life. Let's dive in, shall we?

THE POWER OF A MOTIVATIONAL MINDSET

You were not created just to be average. Those who are average have chosen to be. We were all created to be exceptional, and it's our job to make sure that we reach our full potential. But what if we have no motivation to do exactly that?

I am sure we've all felt motivated at some point in our lives, but for some reason, that motivation may have started to decline and disappear altogether. Sometimes, when we go through difficult times or feel like we failed at something, it's easy to struggle to get back up again. And that's okay. It's okay to not feel okay after a setback. What's important is that we learn how to recover from the setback.

I know it's easy for me to say, but in reality, it's quite difficult to get ourselves out of that slump and continue like nothing ever went wrong. The secret to making it look easy is to adopt a motivational mindset.

Before we dive deeper into what that actually means, how science backs it up, and why it matters, let's take a quick look at how two different individuals approach a situation—Sarah, who has a motivational mindset, and Tim, who hasn't mastered it yet.

Sarah and Tim are twins. They had the same upbringing and have gone through similar situations to develop their character. However, the way they approach every problem, especially difficult ones, is different.

The exams are about to start, and they are both quite anxious about them. It's one of the most important academic years and will help decide their future.

Sarah has developed a plan of action to ensure that she spends enough time preparing for each subject and even works in some breaks in between. Although anxious, she feels ready and prepared to take it on. In addition to the study plan, she has weaved in time to get some fresh air and exercise to stay motivated and focused.

Then there's Tim. The additional pressure has caused Tim to creep into his shell a little bit more than usual, and he's choosing to isolate himself from others while he prepares for the exams. He stays in his room and only emerges when it's time to eat or he *really* needs to shower. He takes it day by day and never feels like he has enough time. This has led to severe anxiety and clouded judgment, resulting in him not being able to study properly for the next exam.

Although they both have access to the same resources and face the same problems, Tim is having a much harder time getting a grip on things and staying motivated than Sarah. The beauty of it all is that Tim can have the same experience as Sarah. It really is just a mindset shift.

WHAT'S IN A MINDSET

We all have a specific type of mindset. This is created based on our upbringing, experiences, and beliefs about mindset. The mindset we have influences everything around us, from our daily choices to what we choose to accept, and even what we believe about those around us. It makes up such a big part of who we are that I am convinced it determines our personality traits to some degree. This is why people sometimes blame their personality and insist that *This is just who I am* instead of changing their mindset.

The truth is that we have the power to change our mindset. We don't need to feel stuck and accept mediocrity. Our brains can constantly evolve and adapt if we let them. We have complete control over that. We just need the motivation to change it.

In my first book, *A Growth Mindset For Teens*, I go into detail about a fixed versus a growth mindset. It lays the perfect foundation for understanding mindset.

Being motivated to do something means we will do everything in our power to make sure we achieve what we have set out to achieve. It's the driving force behind everything that we do daily. Most of the time, motivation comes from within. It's a choice that we have to make.

Having a motivational mindset means making motivation a primary decision-maker in your life. You choose to let motivation take the reins regardless of the situation that you are facing. A motivational mindset consists of the following main components:

- **Confidence:** Theodore Roosevelt (n.d.) once said, "Believe that you can, and you're halfway there." Believing in yourself is half the battle. You need to believe in yourself and know that you are amazing and can do whatever you put your mind to.
- **Courage:** Being courageous helps you to try again, even when it feels like you failed the first time. Courage is what pushes you to be better. It's what gets you out of your comfort zone so that you can grow and do something you've never done before to achieve something you've never achieved before.
- **Positivity:** This is such an underrated characteristic to develop. Positivity can turn any bad situation around and help you see the silver lining or create one. When it seems like everything is going wrong, positivity enables you to see possibility.
- **Self-discipline:** This might be a tough one, but it's important to be disciplined. When you're not disciplined, it's more challenging to do something when you don't feel like it. Self-discipline helps you to get started and keep going, even when you don't want to.

- **Strength:** To adopt a motivational mindset, it's necessary to be strong. You need to be able to rise above the negativity and fight off any self-doubt that might try to get you down, because you can overcome anything life throws at you.

As with everything else, there are definitely some misconceptions when it comes to our mindset. Now that we understand what mindset is, let's dive a little deeper into some common misconceptions about mindset and motivation and what the truth is:

- **A mindset can't be changed:** We've already briefly touched on this earlier in this section, but I felt it necessary to mention it again. We often feel stuck, like there's nothing we can do about how we see a situation and respond to it. The truth is the exact opposite—we have complete control over our mindset. It can't change overnight, and there is a lot of work that needs to go into it, but if we put in the effort, we can make a change for the better.
- **I just need self-affirmations:** Self-affirmations alone will not help to change a mindset. It might help when you're in the moment, but it's not a long-term solution. Self-affirmations only help in certain circumstances and will have no power if our mindset is not aligned.
- **It's who I am:** Although our mindset plays a massive role in who we are, it's not something that we are born with. We develop a certain type of mindset based on

several factors, and the more we learn it, the stronger it will get.

- **Being rewarded helps motivation:** People often think that they will remain motivated if they are constantly rewarded for their efforts. Although this may be true in some situations, different kinds of motivation will apply to different situations. You won't be able to adopt a motivational mindset by just rewarding yourself for everything.

- **Motivation is a characteristic:** Many people believe that motivation is part of our innate traits and that you can't cultivate motivation if you don't have that characteristic. It's not a personality trait at all. Motivation can either be intrinsic (coming from within) or extrinsic (received from outside), but everyone can be motivated. We may all just have different things that drive the motivation.

- **To be successful, you only need to be motivated:** Motivation is an essential aspect of being successful, but we need a lot of other skills and strategies to be successful. Resilience, time management, and effective coping mechanisms are great examples.

Activity One: Motivational Mindset Components

We briefly described some critical components of a motivational mindset, but many other elements encompass motivation and a motivational perspective. For the first exercise, I want you to really think about the critical components of motivation discussed earlier in the chapter, such as confidence, courage, positivity, self-discipline, and strength. There could be others, depending on what's important to you when it comes to feeling motivated.

Grab a pen and paper or open your note app, and write down three key components of motivation that you think are most important. There is no right or wrong answer here—just figure out what motivation means to you. Once you've written down three of them, explain why those specific three stand out for you. Here are some additional ones not mentioned earlier to get your train of thought started: optimism, bravery, high self-esteem, self-confidence, strong sense of purpose, decision-making skills, reflectivity, and persistence.

Understanding what is most important to you and identifying what you need to work on will make it a lot easier to build the roadmap to achieving a motivational mindset.

THE BRAIN BEHIND THE DRIVE

We won't go into too much detail about the science behind motivation. Still, it is helpful to understand some basics so that you can realize that it is possible to become highly motivated, even if you've been feeling unmotivated your whole life.

In a nutshell, the psychology of motivation can be measured using four main components: behavior (which includes things such as how quickly we do something, the persistence we show to complete it, our facial expressions, and the effort we put in), psychophysiology (which includes bodily functions like the hormones we secrete, emotions we feel and show, pupil size, and heart rate), neural activation (this is a lot more technical and out of scope, but at a high level, you need to know that different regions in the brain activate when we are faced with other circumstances), and level or levels of engagement (such as showing interest in the task at hand, being focused, and contributing meaningfully where possible).

There are two types of motivation: extrinsic motivation and intrinsic motivation.

- **Extrinsic motivation:** This is motivation that we may get from external sources and also typically comes with external physical rewards. Although still a necessary type of motivation, it is often short-lived if it doesn't turn into intrinsic motivation.

  - For example: This type of motivation in action could be explained using exams. If you haven't been doing your best, and your parents promise that they will buy you a new phone if your marks improve by at least 5% overall, your reason for being motivated comes from your parents and the promise that you will receive something you really want as a reward.

- **Intrinsic motivation:** This motivation comes from within and is usually accompanied by personal emotional rewards rather than physical ones. It becomes part of who we are as a person because it fuels us on every level.

○ For example: Someone who enjoys running is motivated to push themselves to run further and improve their time. The only reward they receive is knowing that they are improving themselves.

It should come as no surprise that our motivation and what drives it will change as we grow older or face different situations. We won't be motivated by the same things in 10 years that we are now because other things will occupy us. So, remember that this may change in a few years when deciding what is worth feeling motivated for.

Activity Two: A List of Things

I love making lists, because it helps to organize thoughts logically. For this activity, I want you to list a few things that motivate you and a few that don't.

Grab a pen and paper or whatever method you prefer to make notes. Before writing anything down, think about a few things that motivate you. Make a list of at least five things that encourage you. These can be a combination of intrinsic and extrinsic factors, or you can focus on just one—just come up some things like setting a new personal record, obtaining a personal best with weightlifting, or receiving money as a reward. Once you've done that, think about and list five things that don't motivate you at all. These can be things that are simply not important to you, like getting a new phone or fitting into a specific size shirt.

Once you've made these lists, reflect on why these things motivate you or why they don't and write them down.

This activity will help you to see what's important to you and what you couldn't care less about when it comes to feeling motivated. This is pivotal to the journey ahead.

As an extra step, choose one of the aspects that motivate you and brainstorm ways to use it in other aspects of your life to feel more motivated.

Activity Three: Motivation Board

This is like a vision board, but we'll call it a motivation board. Creating one you can look at all day is fun to make and helps you reap the benefits when things start getting tough.

You can create a motivation board in any way you can get creative. Choose what you prefer, whether physical or electronic. What you choose for your motivation board is also up to you. They can be quotes, pictures, words, or a combination of all. You can even paint or draw if that's your thing. Whatever you choose, get all of it together.

The elements for your motivation board should be things that actually motivate you. You can use the list you made in Activity Two to help you with ideas if you need them. Make sure that your motivation board is appealing for you to look at. Take your time and really plan it out before you finalize it. Once you're done, make sure you put it somewhere where you can see it every single day.

Creating a motivation board is going to help you find the momentum and will to keep going—to chase your goals when you feel like giving up. We all have bad days when we need an extra push in the right direction.

CONNECT THE DOTS BETWEEN WANTING AND GETTING

Have you ever felt like it's nearly impossible to achieve some of your goals while other people seem to achieve theirs effortlessly?

There can sometimes be a difference in what we want to achieve and what we end up achieving. A few factors can influence the relationship between the two, and we end up not getting the results we want. Understanding this concept and knowing how to navigate it can make all the difference.

The recipe to success is to incorporate motivation into goal setting. To be successful, you can't have one without the other. We will go into goal setting and the steps to set SMART goals in Chapter 5. For now, let's cover some fundamentals.

Do you sometimes feel like you just don't have enough time in the day to do everything you want or need to do? You're not alone in that. It's something that we all deal with daily. The problem is not the amount of time we have in a day because other people get to do all those things and more. The issue is our lack of motivation. Without motivation, getting anything more done than the bare minimum is difficult.

The Goal Setting Theory, developed by Edwin A. Locke, suggests that when we set specific goals that we want to reach, this motivates us to commit to the task at hand and achieve our goals (Hashmi, 2022). I think the biggest problem we have is getting started. I've seen this in my own life. I will put something off for weeks because I don't have the motivation for it, but once I get started, it's difficult to stop! There's a new fire that makes me want to knock it out of the park and do even more.

That's the big difference between people who effortlessly achieve their goals and those who struggle to do so—motivation. Or rather, the absence thereof. Luckily, this whole book is dedicated to helping you adopt a motivational mindset!

It's easy to say, "Just be motivated," but there are many pitfalls that make it difficult to achieve our goals while staying motivated. Let's look at some of the most common obstacles and how to manage them effectively.

- **Allowing negative thinking patterns:** We've all been victims of negative thoughts. You know the ones. *I can't do this, I'm not good enough, I'll never achieve my goals,* or one of my personal favorites: *My dreams are too big.* When we allow these negative thoughts to take root in our minds, they can block us from achieving anything, which cultivates even more negative thoughts.

  ○ As soon as you realize that your thoughts are leaning toward the negative side, stop them immediately and replace them with more positive thoughts: *I was born to be exceptional, I am good enough, I can achieve anything I put my mind to,* and *my dreams are the perfect size because I can achieve them.*

- **Feeling lazy:** This is not meant to call you out at all. We all deserve to be lazy sometimes, but some of us take it too seriously.

  - We need to put in the work if we want to see results. That does mean working on our goal instead of watching a Netflix series or spending hours on social media.

- **Lack of confidence:** Not being confident in your abilities can cause major delays in getting anything done. A lack of confidence can be caused by negative thinking and vice versa. But it could also be due to previous experiences.

  - Knowing your worth and what you can do will help keep you motivated. Make sure that you are aware of your strengths and areas of improvement.

- **Not being focused:** This is directly connected to being motivated, so it should come as no surprise that it made it onto the list. Stay focused. There will always be other things that will ask for your attention, and they might all still be necessary. So, how do you keep focused?

- Plan your day and set time to focus on certain things in your schedule specifically. We will discuss this in further detail in Chapter 5.

- **Running out of ideas:** Sometimes, we spend so much time trying to achieve something that we eventually run out of ways to make it happen. This lack of creativity can put a hold on our progress.

  - When this happens, the best thing to do is reset and refocus. Take a break and start fresh. Have a brainstorming session with someone you trust that can help get things moving again.

- **Shooting for the moon:** I know there is a famous saying that says that you should shoot for the moon because if you miss, at least you'll land among the stars. Although that is great advice, it's not always the best approach. When we set goals that are far out of reach, it can negatively impact our mindsets. The harder we try, the more we realize that we won't reach our goal, and that may lead to us not trying anymore.

  - We need to focus on setting goals that we can achieve. Yes, they need to be ambitious. But they must also be realistic.

Activity Four: Failed Goals

A failed goal is something you may have set before but didn't or couldn't achieve.

For this activity, I want you to think about a goal that you've set in the past but didn't achieve. There is no set time frame, but the more recent it is, the better. Once you have a goal in mind, write it down in as much detail as possible. Include when you set the goal, why you set the goal, and when it became a failed goal (i.e., When did you stop working toward it?).

Once you have that level of detail, I want you to reflect on the reasons why this goal was unattainable. Think of the factors that may have affected your motivation. You can use the list from the previous section to help you get started.

Reflecting on a scenario where things didn't go exactly as planned helps us to identify factors that we may be able to change in the future to prevent it from happening again.

Activity Five: Tracking Motivation Levels

For this activity, we're just going to track our motivation levels for a week and see how it changes throughout the week.

Think about something small that you know you can achieve within a week. It doesn't have to be linked to any long-term plans. Choose something you've meant to do, like reading a new book or finishing a Lego build.

Write down the goal and be as specific as possible. It has to be done within a week, so don't choose something that may take you longer. Once you have your goal, write down the steps you will follow to achieve it. This could be a bunch of smaller goals to accomplish the primary objective. The easiest way to do this is to decide what you want to achieve per day.

As the week goes by, note down your motivation level whenever you're busy working on your goal. Make sure that you record the time of day, how you're feeling, what the weather is like, whether you've recently eaten, and so on—anything that you think might affect your motivation levels.

At the end of the week, try to see whether there were any patterns in your motivation levels. Perhaps you were the most motivated in the early morning hours or after an afternoon nap.

Knowing when our motivation level fluctuates, when we're at our best, and what influences our motivation levels is key to achieving our goals. We can use this information to help propel us forward and find ways to aid our motivation levels when they seem low.

WHY A MOTIVATIONAL MINDSET MATTERS

There are so many short- and long-term benefits to cultivating a motivational mindset. It affects every aspect of our lives.

Some of the short-term benefits include increased self-esteem, improved mood, more positive feelings, more strength, and more energy.

The long-term benefits include a better perception of who you are and knowing how to present yourself, improved resilience, better decision-making skills, always striving to improve yourself, improved time management, vision for the future, and ultimately inner peace.

Activity Six: Me In Five Years

For this activity, we're going to try and visualize what life would be like in five years without a motivational mindset and with one.

Get your pen and paper or note app, and start with the heading of the activity. Now, I want you to close your eyes and visualize what your life could possibly look like five years from now if you don't adopt a motivational mindset. We've gone through the benefits and why they are necessary, which should help with creating a picture of where those things are missing. Write it down and go into as much detail as possible. Mention what kind of job you will have or what you'll be doing in life (such as studying or not?), where you're living, what kind of lifestyle you're living, and so on.

Once you've done that, take a few minutes to reset. When you're ready, I want you to close your eyes again. Now, visualize what your life might possibly look like if you cultivate and adopt a motivational mindset. Again, go into as much detail as possible.

When you're done, draw up a comparison and focus on the key differences.

Visualizing the future and realizing the difference a mindset shift makes can help you to achieve everything you want in life and more. Keep your vision of yourself in five years (with a motivational mindset) and refer back to it whenever you need some additional motivation.

Activity Seven: Role Models

A role model is someone who exhibits characteristics and skills that we admire and would want to be more like.

Think about a few people that you look up to and admire with a motivational mindset. These people are generally very optimistic and successful. Write down a few specific traits that you admire about them.

Having a list of role models (and traits you aspire to have) is a great way to feel more motivated to improve and become a better version of yourself.

Activity Eight: Personal Affirmations

We all need a collection of personal affirmations so that we can pick ourselves up when life knocks us down or when the negative thoughts start taking over. A personal affirmation is something that you believe of yourself but may forget in the moment, and you're just reminding yourself. It can also be something you aspire to but don't believe just yet.

It's time to (yes, you guessed it) grab a pen and paper or your note app!

Make a list of a few personal affirmations that you can use in any situation. I have included a short list below just to get the creative juices flowing, but feel free to use your own. They have to be personal and mean something to you. When you write them down, use the present tense to make them real, not something you used to or aspire to be.

- I am good enough.
- I can do this.
- I can get through anything because I am resilient.
- I have achieved so much, and I am proud of myself.
- I bring a lot to the table.

Having a few personal affirmations in your back pocket will help a lot when you're feeling down, and no one is there to pick you up. Never underestimate the power of a simple "I am amazing!"

CHAPTER 1 SUMMARY

- Our mindset influences how we conduct ourselves daily.
- The five main components of a motivational mindset are confidence, courage, positivity, self-discipline, and strength.
- There are a few misconceptions around mindset that are important to understand to be able to change our mindset.

- Two types of motivation exist: extrinsic motivation, which is driven by outside forces and rewards, and intrinsic motivation, which comes from within and is a lot more personal.
- Our level of motivation and what motivates us changes as we get older.
- Just striving for a better or successful life is not enough. We need the motivation to chase those dreams.
- There are a few common barriers that prevent us from actualizing our dreams and visions. It's important to pay close attention to these and avoid them.
- There are many short- and long-term benefits to cultivating a motivational mindset.

After going through this chapter, are you ready to be a Sarah instead of a Tim?

In the next chapter, we will explore how you can tap into your unique skills and ambitions to ignite your inner drive. We will dive into how to understand your own potential, recognize your strengths, have a vision for the future, and avoid negative influences in your life.

DISCOVERING YOUR INNER DRIVE

Have you ever really wanted to do something but couldn't find that drive to get started or keep it going? It might be because you haven't fully discovered your inner drive and how you can use it to propel yourself forward.

We will have a look at some of the ways you can discover your unique skills and spark that inner drive that will motivate you, no matter what. You have a lot of potential; we just need to unlock it.

It's story time again. This time, we'll look at Mary and Mark. They are best friends, but sometimes, it's difficult for Mary to communicate with Mark because of his mindset.

Mary has done a lot of self-reflection and knows exactly where her strengths lie. She uses this knowledge to pick herself up whenever things don't go as planned and to come up with a plan b. No matter what, she manages to always turn a situation around for the better. She has a clear vision of what she's working toward and knows how to get there.

Mark, on the other hand, really struggles with knowing his worth and has spent little to no time with himself. He has a vague idea of his strengths but hasn't explored them or seen how good they are. He struggles to plan ahead, even if it's just a week or two. His lack of vision makes it difficult for him to know what direction he wants to go, and he falls into negative behaviors and thinking patterns.

It's challenging for Mary to help him navigate these scenarios since his mindset is very fixed, and he can't seem to change it. It has had quite a big impact on their friendship because Mary feels like it's affecting her personal growth.

If only Mark had the tools in this chapter to help him discover these strengths and inner drive to move forward.

DIG DEEP TO KNOW YOUR WORTH

Did you know you need to understand your potential before becoming a better version of yourself? Just hear me out quickly. Without the in-depth knowledge of what you're capable of, how will you know what you can actually achieve? How will you know that there is, in fact, a better version of yourself?

Understanding your own potential isn't something people talk about often, but it's so important. At the same time, you need to be aware of your shortcomings so that you can put measures in place to avoid or overcome them in the process of bettering yourself.

We all have special skills and traits that make us unique. Sometimes, we choose to hide these things instead of being unapologetically ourselves. In other instances, we may not even be aware of what those traits or skills are.

Being your authentic self is such a rush, but you can only do that when you really know yourself and your worth. Knowing yourself includes knowing what you like and don't like, accepting who you are, having a clear understanding of your beliefs and values, having a vision for your future, and being adaptable, to name a few.

Meg Selig coined the term VITALS to help you with getting to know yourself better (Cooks-Campbell, 2022):

- Values: What do you value in life?
- Interests: What are your interests?
- Temperament: This is mainly focused on where your energy comes from (i.e., whether you are an introvert, an extrovert, or a combination of both).
- Around-the-clock activities: This is whatever you enjoy doing daily.
- Life-mission and goals: What gives your life meaning?
- Strengths and weaknesses: This should focus on hard skills such as specific knowledge, and soft skills such as emotional intelligence.

You'll notice that none of these include any form of external validation. That's because who you are and your self-worth should not be linked to what others think or say about you or any other external factors such as your appearance, job, relationship status, or even money you have. When we link our self-worth to external factors, it can change daily if any of those factors shift slightly.

We need to look inward for our self-worth and know without a doubt what qualities make us unique. By having a high level of self-worth, we can reap benefits such as improved problem-solving skills (solving them with confidence), making decisions easier, meeting our own needs, knowing our limits, and maintaining relationships.

Activity Nine: Qualities That Make Me Proud

As we've established, we all possess certain traits or qualities that make us unique or special. Even if one or two is the same as the next person's, your combination of qualities is unique. For example, it's not uncommon to have a high emotional intelligence. It may be unusual to have it, along with being flexible and having the ability to make a delicious meal out of leftovers. No, these qualities don't always have to be related to each other to mean something!

A quality is something that comes naturally to you and not necessarily something you've learned to do. You might become better at it the more you apply it to your life, but they're an inherent part of your personality.

For this activity, write down five traits or qualities that make you proud. Think hard about this one, and make sure you choose the ones you are most proud of. Once you've done that, think about two instances where these qualities or traits have been beneficial to you. They may not all apply to the same events, and you can use your discretion whether you want to use two different events for all five or just reflect on two events where most of them were used.

Now, we're going to do something that we haven't done in the activities up until this point. I want you to take your findings and discuss them with someone that you can trust so they can also give their input or feedback. They may point out something that you missed.

Knowing which traits or qualities make you unique is great, but also understanding how they feed into your daily life is even better. It helps us understand the value of these qualities and how different our lives could have been without them.

UNCOVER YOUR SPECIAL SKILLS

Skills are a little different from qualities. These are things that we have been taught to do from a very young age. Although we learn to do these, some people might struggle to pick up certain skills more than others. Just like with qualities, the more we apply them and learn more about them, the better we will become at them.

Knowing what your own skills are is pivotal to your growth and future success. These skills, together with our inherent qualities, are what set us apart from others and will ultimately determine whether we get the job over the next person with similar skills.

Something that can really help with uncovering your special skills is self-awareness. This means having a good knowledge of your qualities, desires, beliefs, triggers, motives, and feelings—in other words, knowing yourself inside and out—knowing what makes you tick.

There are two different kinds of self-awareness:

- **Private self-awareness:** This involves a lot of introspection and knowing what affects us internally. This is the type of self-awareness we need to work on most to determine our special skills, unique traits, and qualities.
- **Public self-awareness:** This means to be aware of how others see you. It helps us to decide what behavior is and isn't appropriate when we are around others. It's a good type of self-awareness, but it could be quite dangerous when it starts leaning more toward the self-conscious side (i.e., being too aware and too careful of how we act around others).

Some benefits of being more self-aware include improved self-confidence, cultivating a growth mindset, and being more optimistic.

Now that we've covered self-awareness, I've included a few ways in which you can determine your own special skills and strengths.

- **Take a test:** One of the easiest and quickest ways to find out what your strengths are is to take a test. There are many around that you can leverage, online and in-person. Make sure you use a reputable source if you decide to go the online route.

- **Ask around:** Have an open conversation with the people you spend the most time with, and ask them what some of your strengths are. Be open to feedback and don't deny something if they identify it as a strength. If someone says something that surprises you, ask them to elaborate on why they say it is a strength of yours. They won't be able to provide you with an exhaustive list, but it's also a good place to start.

- **Identify what you're passionate about:** By knowing what drives you, strengths become easier. You are more likely to succeed in something and cultivate it as a strength when you are passionate about it. Knowing what you are passionate about and what you enjoy doing can help you uncover some hidden skills.

- **Pay attention to your day:** The instances during the day when we feel that time is really flying by are the times that we are most likely to be using our strengths. This is because using our strengths makes things look and feel more effortless. Note down during the day when things go really well and what skill you're most likely using to make things easier.

It's nice to know what your strengths are in case the question ever comes up, but what's equally important is knowing how to leverage it for both academic and personal gain. Here are some ways you can leverage your strengths in everyday life.

- **Own it:** You need to walk around like you believe these are your strengths. Be proud of what you are good at and look for any opportunity to show it off. Think of some accomplishments involving your strengths that you can share with others when the question comes up.
- **Invest in yourself:** Knowing your strengths is just the first step. It's important to now build on these and become so good at it that you don't even have to think about it anymore. Set goals where you can work on your special skills and improve them even more.
- **Create new habits:** You need to use this new knowledge to build new habits that utilize your skills. Identify any bad or unhealthy habits that you have, and find ways to improve or replace them using your skills.
- **Don't forget to use them:** Whenever you're faced with a situation that might seem a little challenging, go back to your list of strengths and see which ones you can use to make it more manageable.

Activity Ten: Favorite Activities

We all have some things we enjoy doing, and more often than not, these activities involve our strengths and special skills.

Think about some of the activities you enjoy most and make a list. Consider activities you like doing by yourself, with certain friends and family, over the holidays, and so on. Once you've made a list, think about what you are really good at when it comes to these activities. Why do you enjoy them so much?

This activity will help you identify any additional strengths that you may have overlooked when you initially thought about it.

Activity Eleven: Recall a Moment

We shouldn't live in the past; however, when things go really well, it's important to reflect on what, exactly, led to the success.

Think back to a moment when you felt the most effective. This can be in your personal life, school, work, family dynamics, or any other aspect of your life. Try to remember exactly what happened and how you managed the situation. Try to identify the skills that you were using to navigate it.

We can learn from our successes almost as much as we can from our failures. Don't always just focus on what you can learn from what went wrong. You should also reflect on what went right sometimes.

Activity Twelve: Online Strength Assessment

You will find quite a few online strength assessments that can help you identify what you are best at. You can also use it as a second measure for any skills that you're not sure of.

If you don't know where to start, a quick search on the internet will give you quite a few options, such as High 5 Test, Clifton Strength Finder, and Ikigai. Once you have the results, discuss them with a trusted adult who can help explain them. It's also a good sense check in case there are some strengths that you weren't aware of. They will be able to help show you where you demonstrate these skills and how to become more aware of them.

These assessments are developed to pinpoint skills you might not even know.

MAKE YOUR FUTURE VISION CLEAR

You may be wondering at this point why having a future vision is so important. You're still young, there is no way you can decide your entire life right now, right? Well, yes and no.

Having a vision for the future is what helps us to keep moving forward. Without having something we're working toward, we might have a hard time convincing ourselves to get out of bed in the morning, especially when things start becoming difficult. By knowing your vision for the future, you can be more intentional with your actions and what you choose to spend your time on.

Vision does more than just that. It also helps us to decide who we spend our time with, the friends we make, and our daily habits. It drives everything we do. Without vision, we might feel like everything is falling apart.

This doesn't mean that you need to have your whole life figured out now and know when you will retire. It does, however, mean that you need to decide what the tone of your life will be. Will you settle for less than you deserve, or are you going to be exceptional? You can start by setting small goals (which we will explore further in Chapter 5) that encompass your vision and what you hope to achieve.

Before we can get to setting goals, we need to determine what our personal vision is. I have included a few steps below to help you get started:

- **Think about it:** Take some time out where you can be alone, somewhere quiet where you won't be disturbed. Maybe even your favorite coffee shop or a spot in the park. Somewhere where you feel happy and at ease. Allow your mind to wander for a few minutes about what you see yourself achieving in the next 10 years or so, and get it down on paper. Just a paragraph or two should do. Think about everything important to you that motivates you and how you would like others to remember you.
- **Imagine it:** Once you have your paragraph all written down, close your eyes and imagine yourself living that life in 10 years, then decide how you are going to get there based on where you are now. Write down everything that needs to happen and that you need to work on to get there.
- **Get personal:** This is where you need to create a plan. Decide what you are going to do in the short- and long-term to make those things happen. Try a five-year and a one-year plan. You will need to refer back to this often to make sure that it's all still relevant and what your next steps should be, so don't lose it!

Make sure that your vision is clear-cut and easy to understand. When there are any uncertainty or gray areas, it's easier for us to lose motivation because we're not 100% sure exactly what we are chasing. It's not good enough to just know more or less in which direction to run. We need an exact location of where we're off to.

Activity Thirteen: Create a Vision Board

This is such a fun activity—definitely one of my favorites! A vision board is something that visually represents your vision. It's normally a collection of words, affirmations, images, quotes, and objects that are arranged in a visually pleasing way and motivate you to chase your vision.

You can choose what medium you want to use for your vision board and what exactly you want to put on it.

- The first step to creating your vision board is to have a clear idea of what your vision is. If you haven't done that yet, refer back to the section *Make Your Future Vision Clear* and write down your vision.
- Decide how you want to present your vision board (i.e., should it be a physical or a digital vision board? Whiteboard, corkboard, or magnetic board?). Gather all the materials that you will need to bring your vision board to life, everything from markers to glitter or even paint. Whatever you want to use. And don't forget the scissors. If you decide on a digital vision board, get a

program or an app that will help you easily create the board.

- Find everything you need to visually represent your vision. Remember that you can use anything you like: images, words, quotes, objects, and so on. Anything that speaks to your vision. Cut out and prep everything.
- Now it's time for some fun! Start arranging everything you want to add to your vision board. Make sure that the layout inspires you and is visually appealing. It should be something that you would like to look at every day and that will motivate you to chase after it.
- Once you're done, make sure that you put your vision board somewhere you will see it every day. It can be your mirror, your dresser, the fridge, or even your desktop.

When done right, a vision board can propel you forward into the future you've always wanted. If your vision board is not making you feel inspired and motivated, change it! It's not something that should be rigid but flexible.

KEEP AWAY FROM BAD VIBES

It doesn't matter how clear our vision is or how motivated we are; as soon as we start allowing negativity and bad vibes to affect us, we will have a harder time achieving what we want. This is because we are more likely to focus on the negative than on the positive. This is referred to as negative bias and is human nature.

By leaning into negative bias, we often experience certain emotions that can hinder us from moving forward. This includes feeling worried, unworthy, shameful, angry, empty, hurt, and any other emotion you can think of that makes you feel less than what you actually are!

Although it's difficult, we can definitely work on and overcome negative bias. Here are some tricks that I've picked up over the years that I'm sure will help you, too.

- **Be vigilant:** It's important to identify when you are having negative thoughts. As soon as they creep in, you need to recognize it and speak against it. Instead of leaning into the negative thoughts, have grace for yourself and be patient. In the beginning, you might find yourself embracing negative bias quite a lot. As time passes and you get better at recognizing it, it will happen less.
- **Use reframing to change the way you think about things:** Once you identify yourself as having a negative thought, try to replace it with something more positive. You can use your list of personal affirmations from Activity Eight.
- **Keep a gratitude journal:** We tend to underestimate the power of being grateful. Gratitude will change your entire life—trust me.
- **Practice mindfulness:** When we practice mindfulness, we become more aware of our emotions and how to manage them.

Activity Fourteen: Identifying Negative Influence

Most of us have to deal with negative influences daily. One of the key aspects of managing our negative bias is to limit the negative influences.

Reflect on and identify people or situations that have a negative influence on your mindset. If you can't think of anything at the moment, try to identify them as you face them during the day and make a note of it. Once you've identified some, choose one of them and brainstorm some ideas on how you can limit the impact it has. You can definitely focus on more than one if you want to. Rope in an adult or trusted friend to help if you get stuck.

Limiting the impact a negative person or situation has on us can change our day for the better. We often underestimate the power negative influences have in our lives. See how much your day changes once you limit the power of the bad vibes.

Activity Fifteen: Sharing Your Insights

Sharing is always caring.

Approach a trusted friend or adult and share your insights from the previous activities with them. Ask them for their opinion and some additional coping strategies that they may be able to share with you. It's good to learn from others.

CHAPTER 2 SUMMARY

- To become the best version of ourselves, we need to be aware of our potential. We can use the VITALS acronym to help us with self-discovery: values, interests, temperament, around-the-clock activities, life-mission and goals, and strengths and weaknesses.
- Everyone has special skills that make them unique. To identify these skills, we need to become more self-aware.
- Having a vision for the future is vital for growth and motivation. A clear vision ensures that we don't lose motivation.
- Regardless of our motivation, if we allow negative bias to take over, we can quickly lose motivation.

Now that you have a better understanding of your unique skills and your vision board ready, it's time to hone in on some critical skills you need for a motivational mindset: resilience and confidence.

CULTIVATING RESILIENCE AND CONFIDENCE

R esilience and confidence are two of the most crucial skills we need to develop to face life's various challenges. In this chapter, we will explore practical steps for increasing self-esteem, leveraging physical activity, embracing failure, and developing resilience.

To demonstrate the importance of these skills, let's look at two siblings: John and Jamie. Their parents recently got divorced, and they lost their beloved family dog, Oliver, who has been around for more than 10 years. Although they're going through the same ordeal, they each have their own way of dealing with it.

John has recognized that the setbacks can help to propel him forward and make plans for the future. He realized that life is too short not to go after what you want and decided to start making plans to benefit his future self. He goes to the gym every morning to ensure that his mental and physical health both get attention. He also enjoys playing football with his friends over the weekends and spends quite a bit of time in the outdoors when the weather allows. He has tried to invite Jamie, but she hasn't been very keen to go anywhere.

Jamie has decided to cut herself off from all friends and family, except the ones that give her the undivided attention she wants. She has buried herself in self-pity and keeps talking about the good old days when things were right. She likes to look at family photos where everyone, including Oliver, looks happy. She has decided to print a few of these photos and keep them in her room to remind her what things used to be like.

Although everyone might have their own way of dealing with things, some methods are a lot healthier for us than others. In this case, the way Jamie is dealing with it will make it very difficult for her to move forward and set new goals for the future. She might always choose to live in the past. John, on the other hand, has found a good way to deal with his emotions and makes sure that he is still focused on his future self.

No one else is going to make plans for your future self. You need to care enough for your future self to do things now that may benefit them. It is your responsibility to make it happen.

BOOST YOUR SELF-ESTEEM

Two words that are often used interchangeably are self-confidence and self-esteem. Although they may be related, they have slightly different meanings.

Self-confidence is believing in yourself, knowing and believing what you are capable of, and not allowing anything to influence that belief. It is normally based on prior successes and builds trust in yourself about future success. It's your perception of the ability you believe you have.

Self-esteem is more connected to overall self-worth and not necessarily to success. It's about realizing your own value and is not something that can be changed easily; i.e., if you have a high self-worth, it will be very difficult for anyone to convince you otherwise, and vice versa. A very high and a very low self-esteem can both be dangerous. It's better to have just the right amount of self-esteem.

Both self-confidence and self-esteem are necessary for personal success. It's nearly impossible to motivate yourself to achieve something if you don't believe you can do it. It is possible to have one without the other; however, it's ideal to have both. For this section, we will focus on self-esteem.

If you're struggling with self-esteem, you're not alone. The activities in this section will help you build better self-esteem. In addition to that, I have also listed a few things that can help with it below.

- **Positive self-talk:** This is one of the most trusted ways to improve self-esteem. We will explore this in detail in Activity Sixteen.
- **Stop with the comparing:** Comparing yourself to someone else is one of the worst things you can do for your self-esteem. Even if you are twins, you will be

vastly different. We all experience life differently and grow at a different pace. I always use the example of an apple tree and a daisy. They both start in seed form, but they grow at different speeds and purposes. The daisy will grow within a few days, while the apple tree will take years. The daisy brightens someone's day, comes in various colors, and smells nice. The apple tree provides shade, a home for some animals, and fruit to eat. We need both.

- **Learn to say no:** Being a people pleaser means that you say yes to others, whether you want to or not. You choose to put everyone else's needs and happiness above your own. This can lead to low self-esteem and cause unnecessary stress. Learn how to set boundaries and when it's okay to say no.
- **Acknowledge your admirable traits:** There should be a few things that you like or even love about yourself. Whether they are physical attributes, qualities, or characteristics, write them down. It might be a little weird in the beginning, but admitting what you like about yourself is the first step to improved self-esteem.
- **Set boundaries:** Boundaries are crucial to self-esteem. Make sure that you set boundaries in all aspects of your life. This helps to prevent others from taking advantage of you. Make your boundaries clear, and when someone does push the boundaries, remind them of what those are. Sometimes, people can push boundaries unconsciously, so don't assume that they have bad intentions. Boundaries may include only seeing your friends one of the four weekends in a month because

you want to spend the other three with your family, even though your friends want to see you every weekend. These boundaries are personal, and you shouldn't allow others to tell you what they should be.

- **Don't hold on to the past:** We all make mistakes—it's human nature. How we deal with it and move on is what determines whether we learn from it or not. Have grace for yourself when something goes wrong. Don't hold on to the mistake but rather learn from it and commit to not making the same mistake again.

- **Let negative people go:** It sounds terrible to cut people out of your life, but when someone only brings you down, and their whole energy affects you negatively, there is no reason for you to keep them around. You don't have to cut them out completely, but be very selective about how and when you spend time with them.

- **Try new things:** Getting out of your comfort zone is an excellent way to show yourself that you are capable of more than you think. Try something new. Go with your friend to a pottery class, even if you're not the most creative person. Take ballroom dancing classes even though you're awkward and can't dance. By involving yourself in activities you don't think you can partake in, you can improve your self-esteem. Even if you don't succeed, it will be a lot of fun!

- **Spend time with people who are healthy for you:**
  Make sure that you are surrounded by people who are
  good for your mental health. They will always see and
  bring out the best in you. Whenever you're around
  them, you will feel good and happy, like you can
  conquer anything. They will often say nice things about
  you (to your face and behind your back) and tell you
  how amazing you are. When you find them, spend as
  much time with them as you can. These are your
  people.

Having great self-esteem will help you succeed at home and
school, improve your mental health, and improve communication skills, which will make it easier to build and maintain
successful relationships. It will be much easier to be your
authentic self, make better decisions, and improve your motivation. These benefits extend into all stages of life.

Activity Sixteen: Positive Self-Talk

Being kind to ourselves is such an important concept that often
gets brushed off. Yes, it's important to be kind to those around
you, but do you know what it means to be kind to yourself?
Positive self-talk helps us to improve our self-esteem by telling
ourselves that we are capable of doing whatever we put our
mind to. More often than not, we don't even realize how we're
talking to ourselves because no one ever made us attentive to it.
If you had to write down everything you told yourself daily,
would you classify it as kind? Would you speak to the person

you love the most in the world in that way? In this activity, we will learn how to put a positive spin on self-talk.

To really get the full benefits of positive self-talk, you need to be able to immediately identify a negative thought and turn it around. This can be difficult in the beginning if you're so used to the negative self-talk. For one entire day, I want you to really focus on the way you speak to yourself. Whenever a negative thought comes up, I want you to write it down.

Once it's on paper, think about whether there are any facts to support the statement. Then, I want you to identify any emotions you might be feeling and why you're feeling this way. Your feelings are probably what made you have negative thoughts, not any facts. Try to find what you can learn from the situation. Then, reframe the negative thought into something positive. Try to find two positive thoughts for each negative thought. I have included an example of reframing in the table below. You can use a similar process to reframe a negative thought.

Negative thought	What are the facts?	How am I feeling and why?	Is there something I can learn from this?	Let's reframe it
Nobody wants to hang out with me.	I've only reached out to Sandra to make plans for this weekend. I have quite a few close friends and family who care for me.	I am feeling rejected and sorry for myself because Sandra didn't want to hang out with me this weekend.	It's not always about me. Sandra might have other plans this weekend, and that's okay. I can make plans with one of my other friends.	I have a lot of people who care about me. There is always someone I can do something with.

Positive self-talk can improve your self-image, change how you deal with setbacks, influence the way you speak about yourself, and help you cope better.

Activity Seventeen: Brag List

I know nobody likes to brag about themselves, but sometimes we need to hype ourselves up. We need to understand what we bring to the table so that we don't accept less than what we deserve. A brag list is a list of accomplishments that we can refer back to whenever we need a pick-me-up.

You're definitely going to need a pen and paper for this one. Take some time to think about accomplishments you are proud of or anything you have achieved. It could be something really big, like winning an award, or something as small as getting an A on an exam. Add anything and everything worth bragging about, no matter how small it may seem. On a day when you're down, it might be exactly what you need.

Don't underestimate what this list can do. A brag list is the perfect thing to give you a confidence boost when you need it. It might also be exactly what you need for some additional motivation now, even if you're not feeling down.

GET MOVING, GET CONFIDENT

I know. Everyone always tells you to exercise because it will make you feel better. I know you've heard it a million times by now. But there is actually scientific evidence that backs this up. That's why everyone is pushing this agenda. Just hear me out.

Those who look after their physical health by exercising regularly and following a balanced diet have better mental health and a lower chance of developing a mental illness (Reed, 2021). This is because the more you exercise and get active, the more serotonin and endorphins your body releases. Serotonin and endorphins make us feel happy and reduce stress.

When we choose not to exercise, we can fall into a vicious cycle of sadness and doing nothing. The more you sit on the couch and do nothing, the worse you feel, and the more you want to sit on the couch and do nothing and feel bad about yourself doing nothing. The cycle feeds itself.

Exercising will also help to get you away from negative thinking patterns because it distracts the mind and releases these good hormones to lift your mood.

It doesn't have to be a lot of hard work, and you can have fun doing it, all while boosting your self-confidence. Choose something that you enjoy doing. The sky is the limit here. It can be anything. Some physical activity is better than none at all.

Taking a walk daily with your dog is a great start. If you don't have a dog, take a walk. There are many other options: cycling, yoga, going to the gym, jumping rope, dancing, and so on. There is something for everyone. Find something that you like and stick to it. You can even rope in some friends to do it with you. In fact, it will help you to commit when you have someone that keeps you accountable.

Here are some of the ways that exercise can improve your self-confidence:

- **It can help you get a better night's rest:** By exercising regularly, you can improve your sleep. The better you sleep, the better you will feel. Seems like a win-win for me.
- **It can be addictive:** The release of endorphins can make you feel so happy that you get addicted to the feeling (in a good and healthy way), which will make you want to do it more and more. The more you exercise, the more endorphins you will release and the happier you will be.
- **It's about the small wins:** When you start exercising, there is a guarantee that you will make gains in one form or another. It won't happen overnight, but if you keep at it, you will definitely see some changes. Seeing progress will help you to stay motivated. You might even start looking the part, which is always a plus.
- **It gives you something to focus on:** When you exercise, it forces your mind to focus on the activity you are performing, and you forget about everything else. This helps you to cope more effectively with any struggles that you may face because you can go back into them with a clear mind.

Activity Eighteen: Physical Activity

Physical activity is anything that gets you moving.

Choose something from the list above or anything else you would like to do, and do it for at least 20 minutes. Once the 20 minutes is over, write down how you're feeling. About 10 minutes after the physical activity, reflect on your mood again and write down any changes. Think about how it has changed versus how you felt before you performed the exercise.

Any form of physical activity should instantly improve your mood and overall demeanor. For long-term effects, you might want to make it a regular occurrence during your week. That's what the next activity is for.

Activity Nineteen: Weekly Exercise Plan

This is how we incorporate regular physical activity into our schedules: We create a weekly exercise plan. For physical activity to be the most effective, there are three components that we need to include in our exercise plan: cardio, strength training, and flexibility.

Cardio should be part of your exercise routine every day. This is anything that increases your heart rate: walking, running, jumping rope, cycling, and so on. Whether the focus for the day is cardio or not, you should use cardio as part of the warm-up. Ideally, cardio should be your focus for one to two days a week.

Strength training involves weight lifting. It doesn't have to be heavy weights—and girls, you won't get massive shoulders and arms from weightlifting once or twice a week, so don't worry about that. Think of anything with weights. Even body weight can work—lunges, push-ups, squats, and other exercises like that. It would be best if you worked this into your exercise plan once to twice a week.

Flexibility ensures proper range of motion. It helps to prevent your muscles from getting too stiff and enables you to perform specific exercises. At least one day of flexibility is essential. Any form of full-body stretching, such as yoga, will do.

In addition to this, you need to ensure that you also work in a few rest days. Your body needs time to rest and recover.

Once you have set up your exercise plan, try to stick to it for a month and then change it up if you need to. By having a plan, you are more likely to be consistent.

TURN FAILURES INTO LESSONS

When we fail at something, it might feel like the end of the world at that moment. And right then, it probably is. But it's important to see the bigger picture before you set up camp there or try to wish it away. I know we live in a world where others don't highlight their failures. We choose to hide them instead, and I always wonder why. We all fail, so why try to hide it?

The beauty of failing is that we can learn something from it. Every time we fail, there is a lesson we can take from it to improve and try again. When we try again, we go in with experience, so we have a bigger chance of succeeding this time. I know that it's difficult to fail at something. It causes this doubt to brew in our minds like, *Can I even do it? Why am I not good enough?* Instead of allowing those negative thoughts to take over, we should reframe them and ask what we can do better or whether we need any additional resources.

Those who are successful have failed many times before they got it right. Ask anyone successful. They will be able to tell you so many stories of how they failed and what those failures taught them. Every failure got them one step closer to success.

Failing, or even the fear of failing, shouldn't stop you. It should be part of the driving force that motivates you to keep going. Let's look at some reframing techniques that can help.

- Use the 4R model: recognize, reevaluate, reorient, and respond.

  o Recognize that you made a mistake or failed and the emotions you're dealing with as a result. That might seem silly, but often, we ignore this vital step. You can't work on something if you're unable to admit that it's there.

  o Reevaluate the situation and analyze any factors that may have contributed to the failure. By knowing what caused it, it's easier to learn from it. Remember to be kind to yourself and others when going through this process.

- ○ Reorient involves identifying any insights or lessons. It naturally flows from the previous step.
- ○ Respond should be obvious. You now implement what you've learned and try again, this time with your newfound knowledge from the previous attempt.

- Remind yourself that you haven't actually failed. You just found another way it won't work. The only time you fail is when you stop trying, so make sure you get back up and try again. When we were kids, we didn't stop trying to ride our bikes after falling for the first time. We got back up and tried again. Maybe not immediately, and that's okay, too. Sometimes we need some time to realign our minds before we try again. Figure out what works for you and do it.
- Get someone that you can turn to for a pep talk every now and then. We all need it, especially when we try multiple times and keep getting the same result. Maybe they can also provide some insights into the problem and identify something you may have missed.

Another thing that really helps to reframe failures into learning opportunities is a growth mindset. I will briefly discuss it here, but you can read and learn more about it in my first book, *A Growth Mindset for Teens*. These books all flow into each other, and I would encourage you to read them all.

Having a growth mindset means that you learn from criticism, embrace challenges instead of shying away from them, persist whenever you're faced with setbacks, and can identify lessons in failures that will help inspire yourself and others as a result.

Activity Twenty: Recalling Failures

By failure, we're referring to a situation where you tried and didn't succeed. Something that you would like to perhaps try your hand at again.

Think about a recent situation where you failed and write the experience down. Use the 4R model in the previous section to dissect the situation and identify the growth opportunities that exist. Discuss this with someone you trust and see whether they can share any additional perspectives and learnings that you may have missed. Once you've had the discussion, reflect on all of it and outline your next steps to try again or learnings you can apply to future situations of a similar nature.

When we are intentional about learning something from our mistakes, we start adopting a growth mindset and live in a world where there are no failures, only opportunities to do better. Be intentional.

STAND STRONG DURING TOUGH TIMES

Resilience is a topic I deal with in most of my books, but it's such an important concept. Once you get it, it will change your life.

Being resilient means you can easily bounce back after going through a difficult time, and it doesn't take you too long to recover. Cultivating resilience doesn't mean that you will never have any setbacks ever again or never have to face challenges. It just means that you have the tools to overcome it quicker with as little damage done as possible. It's a vital skill if you want to be successful in life.

We all have a level of resilience already, but it is possible to improve it. Our level of resilience is based on the challenges we've had to face in the past and how we dealt with them, what support we had, and what we learned from the experiences.

Here are three things you can do today to help improve your resilience:

- **Build a support network:** Having people around you who can support you no matter what is crucial for resilience. They will help you see your worth when you struggle to.
- **Practice mindfulness daily:** Be mindful and intentional with everything you do. Make sure that you notice the small things that make your day great, like the flowers on the windowsill at your favorite coffee shop or the birds chirping in the park.

- **Focus on self-care**: This one might seem obvious, but a lot of us neglect it. Make sure that you take care of yourself, physically and emotionally. Someone who takes care of themselves feels better about who they are and what they can accomplish than someone who neglects that part of their lives.

The great thing about resilience is that it's good for more than just dealing with setbacks. Some other benefits include learning how to deal with change, not giving up on your dreams, knowing that nothing is too big to overcome, feeling like you're part of something bigger through your support network, and the ability to love yourself.

Activity Twenty-One: Identify a Challenge

The reality is that there will always be another challenge that we need to face. Just when we get through one storm, another will already be brewing somewhere else. The storms may not all be the same in magnitude, but they will be constant, and it's essential to identify them and learn how to effectively deal with them.

For this activity, I want you to think about a challenge you may face right now. Using what you learned about your skills and traits in the previous chapters, brainstorm some ways that you can effectively handle it.

By brainstorming solutions, you take some of the "what if"s out of the equation. Preparing for something helps us perform better instead of just "seeing how this goes."

Activity Twenty-Two: Mindfulness

Mindfulness means to be completely present in the moment. You choose to savor the moment for what it is instead of thinking about the past or the future. We can use mindfulness activities for many reasons. One of the reasons I like using them is when I'm feeling a little stressed and overwhelmed.

We will be looking at some mindfulness breathing that you can practice whenever you're feeling a little stressed. You can do basic breathing techniques that involve just being in a comfortable position and focusing on your breathing with your eyes open or closed. I want to go through the technique called box breathing, which is great for stress relief and helps with concentration.

Find a quiet place, free from distractions and noise. Start by sitting in an upright and comfortable position, making sure that your feet are flat on the floor. Gently place your hands in your lap, palms facing toward the ceiling.

You're going to be inhaling, holding your breath, exhaling, and holding again for four seconds each time. This is where the name of the technique comes from. Start by exhaling slowly through your mouth for four seconds, making sure that all of the oxygen is out of your lungs (or as much as you can breathe out). Hold it for four seconds, then breathe in for four seconds until your lungs are full of air, and hold your breath again for four. Be conscious of how the air feels as it enters and leaves your lungs. Really focus on the breathing and the sensations you are experiencing. You can practice box breathing for about five minutes or longer if you need to.

Box breathing can help regulate some of your body functions and reduce stress. It's an excellent technique to use to clear some clutter and destress.

Activity Twenty-Three: Past Lessons on Resilience

I know we're looking at the past a lot, but there are valuable lessons that you may not have noticed before that are essential to your growth journey.

I want you to think back on a past challenge that you've overcome and what it taught you about resilience. Whether you bounced back fast or whether it took a while to recover, reflect on that and identify what you could have done differently if you had the knowledge you have now.

Apply the knowledge that you are getting to ensure that it sticks. Knowledge without action won't make any difference in your life. We can always learn something from a situation, especially when it all goes wrong.

CHAPTER 3 SUMMARY

- Many of us struggle with low self-esteem. Self-esteem is about knowing your value. We need to work on our self-esteem for the benefit of our future selves.
- Some ways to boost self-esteem include saying no, getting out of our comfort zone, and being kind to ourselves about the past.
- We can use positive self-talk to help us build better self-esteem.
- Physical exercise can help us cope better with what life throws at us and improve our self-esteem and confidence. It doesn't have to be running or going to the gym. There are various types of physical activity that you can try out. Find something that works for you.
- We only fail when we stop trying. Everything else is a lesson we learn. When we learn from our failures, we can do better next time. It's okay to not succeed the first (or even the tenth) time.
- Resilience is a crucial skill to help us recover and move on from failures. We can cultivate better resilience through mindfulness, having a support network, and taking care of ourselves, to name a few.

Now that we've covered some critical skills let's uncover some passions and interests that you might not know you have! By exploring creative outlets and finding inspiration, we can enrich our lives and even set the stage for future career paths.

NURTURING YOUR PASSIONS

Knowing what your passions are and nurturing them is the next step in our journey. These passions can easily help you decide what you want to do one day. Choosing a career you enjoy is vital, so why not one of your passions?

When we start exploring the things that we are passionate about, we become happier and feel more fulfilled daily. These passions feed our overall well-being in such a powerful way.

To demonstrate what an impact this can make, let's look at two friends who approach it differently: Emily and Jake.

Emily has been putting in the work to understand her passions since she was much younger. Her parents encouraged her to explore different activities, physical and creative, and by now, she has a good idea of what she enjoys. Even with this knowledge, she still tries new things in case there is something else that she can add to her list of interests. She found a love for painting the first time her mom brought home finger paint and some paper, and she is part of the art community, where she receives constant support and feedback on her work. This helps her to improve techniques and build her confidence.

Jake is not that keen to try new things. He started football in primary school, and that's all he's ever known. He dedicates all his time to football because he's unsure what else to explore. Although he enjoyed football when he was younger, it no longer fulfills him in the same way, and it's clear that there is a void. Instead of trying to explore new interests, he immerses himself in what he already knows.

There is nothing wrong with sticking to what you know, but it may lead to an unfulfilling life because you're not tapping into your full potential. In this chapter, I will help you explore some potential interests you might have that you don't even know about.

FREE YOUR CREATIVE SIDE

Everyone doesn't have to be an artist to be creative. Everything we do has a form of art to it. The key is to find what makes you tick and unleash it so that you can become the best version of yourself.

You might be wondering why creativity is so important. I have listed a few reasons below, but this is definitely not an exhaustive list.

- Creativity challenges and engages our minds to find new ways of thinking.
- Creativity makes it a lot easier to absorb and remember new knowledge.
- Creativity helps us to think outside of the box and break old thinking habits.
- Creativity helps us connect with our inner self, helping us identify what's unique and special about us.
- When performed in a group setting, creativity helps to join us and overcome barriers or biases.
- Exploring creativity improves problem-solving skills.
- Being creative creates room for curiosity.
- Creativity helps to keep the mind active.
- Creativity also allows us to express our feelings when normal words fail us.
- Being creative can cultivate better resilience.
- Creativity allows us to feel free and joyful.

Doesn't that sound amazing? I'm glad you're on board! The hardest part is getting started. Being creative is not always just about drawing. There are so many different ways to find and express your creativity. Once you know what you like and what you don't like, it's easy to find new things to do. The sky really is the limit here! There is no one-shoe-fits-all.

To help you get started, I've listed a few ideas below that you can try out. Some are activities you can try, and some are tips to get into creative mode.:

- **Avoid all digital devices:** Not for a very long time, just an hour or so. When we are so engrossed in technology and social media, we teach our brains that it's okay to be lazy. Pulling away from this allows our brains to think creatively and get busy with things that stimulate us.

- **Cook up a storm:** Some people can get very creative in the kitchen. Why not give it a go? Offer to make dinner and see what you can come up with! Definitely ask your parents for help, if needed.

- **Dabble your toe in doodling:** This is probably one of my favorite things to do when I'm stressed or need some creativity to flow. Get a notebook and some pens (I love the felt tip pens), and allow your imagination to take over. A doodle doesn't always have to be a full picture. You can just draw a few lines, circles, flowers, or something completely abstract.

- **Explore the unknown:** Getting stuck in a routine is very bad for your creativity. Change up your routine and try something new. Instead of walking the same road when you go out, try a different route—even if it's a little further.

- **Have some fun:** Go back to being a child. Have a fun few minutes at the park where you kick the leaves, see how high you can go on the swings, and go down the slide. Having fun will free your mind and open it to new ideas.

- **Take a walk:** Nature is good for more than just providing fresh air. It can also clear your mind and inspire creativity. Nature is beautiful, and there is a lot you can do in nature. You can collect twigs and leaves to create a masterpiece, get snapping with a camera, or even draw using nature as inspiration. Taking a walk will definitely get the creative juices flowing.
- **Try journaling:** This is a great way to process your thoughts and feelings. The more in touch we are with these, the easier it will be to get creative. There are various journals available online to purchase, and it doesn't always just have to be a *Dear Diary* situation. Have a look on Amazon if you're looking for a themed journal, like a gratitude journal or book journal.
- **The usual suspects:** There are, of course, some of the more well-known methods, such as drawing, painting, or writing. Don't forget these golden oldies—they are still good!

Don't be limited by the items on the list. They are just to get you going. Something like gardening is also a great way to spark creativity if that's something you enjoy. Maybe even browse in the craft section or a DIY store for some inspiration on what you can do to get creative.

Activity Twenty-Four: Getting Creative

We're going to get into the writing and drawing for this activity just to see how it feels. You'll never know unless you try it.

I want you to choose between doodling and journaling. If you've tried one of them already, give the other a go. You can also do both if you want to. Get some pen and paper and just spend 15 minutes on the activity. Do whatever comes to mind. You can journal about your day, the challenges you faced, what you are grateful for—anything at all. If you're doodling, choose something you've always wanted to try and draw. It can even be a little comic strip. It doesn't have to be super professional and impressive. The aim is not to create a masterpiece but to spend some time getting creative.

By taking 15 minutes out of your day to do something that eases the mind, you will be more relaxed for the rest of the day and be able to make better decisions.

Activity Twenty-Five: Creative Problem-Solving

Creative problem-solving helps us to explore potential solutions for problems, even when a problem is not defined. It creates a space for open-ended solutions that are less structured.

Think about any problem that you need to solve, big or small. When you're looking at the problem, try to rephrase it as a question. When we refer to it as a problem, we might see it as a potential obstacle. By reframing it as a question, we can start thinking about solutions.

Start thinking about possible solutions. They don't all need to sound possible. The idea is to come up with as many solutions as you can in response to the problem and then create a short-list of those solutions that are viable to implement. All you need to do now is choose the most feasible one.

Document the process that you went through and how you eventually got to a final answer so that you can refer back to it. You can use mind maps or any other creative method to do this.

Creative problem-solving helps us to see the whole picture and explore possible solutions we may not have thought about otherwise.

Activity Twenty-Six: Sharing Is Caring

Whether you like to talk to other people about your problems or not, sharing really is caring. We've been placed among others to be able to carry each other's burdens. Don't feel like you can't share your problems, concerns, difficulties, or findings with those around you.

Identify a trusted friend or adult with whom you would like to share your creative work and ask them to give you feedback. Any form of feedback should be constructive. Remember that being creative is all about perspective. So, they might not resonate with your creative work, and that's okay.

Sharing our findings and working with other people allows us to bond with them and get their perspective in case we missed anything.

DIVE INTO INTERESTS AND HOBBIES

Do you have a hobby that you get to practice regularly? Hobbies and interests can really help us destress and enjoy life more. If you don't have a hobby, or you don't have a lot of time to spend on it, you need to make a plan.

When we spend time taking care of ourselves by engaging in hobbies and leisurely activities, we also look after our mental health. Hobbies can improve our self-esteem, mood, and confidence. It also helps us to feel like we've accomplished something because we get to spend our time on something we enjoy, whether we're good at it or not.

There are several hobbies that you can try out, some hobbies you probably don't even know exist! You need to find something that you really enjoy and appreciate. Otherwise, you won't feel like doing it and won't make time for it. Here is a list of some hobbies you might want to try out:

- **Bird watching:** This might sound boring, but it's quite a fun hobby to take on. There are so many different bird species to see. Take a day to just spend in nature, watching the various birds. Soon you will start recognizing them by their call.
- **Collecting:** The great thing about collecting is that there really are no rules. You can choose what you want to collect. I personally collect books because they look beautiful on my bookshelf, and I get to read some of them. You can collect anything that strikes your fancy. Think Lego, seashells, figurines, comic books, board

games, or even rocks. If there is something that you would like more of in a variety of forms and colors, do it!

- **Cooking:** This is something that I never thought I would enjoy, but once I started getting into it, I couldn't stop! I was signing up for cooking classes in no time and started baking not long after. You can play around with a lot of different flavors when it comes to cooking and add your own flare to any dish.

- **Dancing:** Nobody said you had to be good at it. There are so many different dance styles that I'm sure you'll find one you enjoy. You could start in your room when no one is watching and progress from there.

- **DIY activities:** There are so many that fall within this category, but think candle making, pottery, or even jewelry design. They all unleash your creative side as well, so it's a two-for-one deal!

- **The outdoors:** Spending time outdoors is a great way to connect with nature and have a good time. Hiking and camping are excellent activities to take on. Grab a few friends and start a hiking club.

- **Photography:** There is something truly special about capturing a moment in time. Getting into photography can be a little pricey the deeper you go into it, but in the beginning, all you really need is a smartphone and an interest in taking beautiful snapshots. And you can choose what you want to photograph. It doesn't have to be people. You can do nature, art, or even studio shooting.

- **The stars:** Astronomy is a very interesting field, and there is so much to learn. Have you always had an interest in the stars, moon, and planets? Why not give it a go? You don't have to be an astronaut one day.
- **Sports:** There are so many different sports that you can try including golf, mountain biking, football, tennis, and fencing. Check out the clubs in your area and join one!
- **Swimming:** This is such a great hobby, and you can always improve on it. Not only is it fun, but it also gives you a full-body workout. It really is a win-win situation.
- **Writing:** This might be a hidden talent that you didn't know you had. Doesn't have to be a novel or a book. You can try your hand at poems, journaling, or even blogging.

I know that the biggest problem is not finding a new hobby. It's finding the time to engage in it. Whenever we need extra time, the first thing we sacrifice is our hobbies. Why do we do that? Why not focus on ourselves?

Hobbies are meant to be enriching, and they should help us develop ourselves. That should be reason enough to want to spend time on them. We need to reframe our minds and not see a hobby as just something we pursue in our free time or that's a nice-to-have. Schedule it into your day, and don't cancel it if something else comes up (unless that something else is significant). Indulge in your hobbies, and you will remain fulfilled for longer.

Activity Twenty-Seven: Exploring New Hobbies

Finding a new hobby can be difficult because you never know what to actually look into and how to get started.

Using the information in the previous section and your advanced internet search skills, find three hobbies you may be interested in taking on. Research how to get started, what you need, and whether there are any clubs or classes in your area for it.

Doing the research and knowing how to get started can help you to put things into action.

Activity Twenty-Eight: Practicing New Hobbies

The next step is to make time to engage in your hobby.

Choose one of the hobbies you listed above that you want to commit to for the next month. Schedule at least one hour a week to spend on your new hobby for a month. At the end of each week, reflect and journal the impact of practicing your new hobby and your overall happiness.

DRAW INSPIRATION FROM THE WORLD

Skill is essential, but it will only get you that far. You need something that inspires you to reach the next level. The more encouraged you are, the more motivation you will have. Inspiration doesn't always have to come from sources that make sense, like a role model. You can't control what inspires you—it just happens. That doesn't mean that there aren't a few things you can do to help it or find it.

- **Add new music to your playlist:** Music can inspire us. Try to add a different genre to your playlist than what you normally listen to.
- **Redecorate:** Sometimes, our environment can hinder our inspiration. Try to redecorate your space and see what a difference it makes.
- **Read a book:** Books contain so much knowledge, and they help challenge our minds to think differently in certain situations.
- **Take a break:** I know it's nice to be busy and always on the move, but sometimes you need to make time to rest.
- **Use mindfulness:** Mindfulness is a powerful tool for various reasons. It can help you to refocus on what's important and focus on what needs to be done.
- **Visit a museum:** A museum is full of artifacts and pieces of art that can spark inspiration and creativity. Use other people's work to inspire you.
- **Walk in nature:** Taking a nature walk can be very inspirational. We will explore this in Activity Twenty-Nine.

When we're inspired, it can help us generate new ideas and propel our personal growth because we strive for more. We know what we want from life and run after it.

Activity Twenty-Nine: Nature Walk

A nature walk is just a walk in the outdoors, preferably where you are surrounded by nature.

On a day when it's nice out, put on some walking shoes and take a walk. Take a journal, camera, or phone with you and photograph or write about anything that inspires you on your walk.

Using nature is one of the easiest and most cost-effective ways to run after inspiration.

Activity Thirty: Do Some Research

Research is an excellent way to gain more knowledge on a certain subject. There's so much information out there on almost anything you can think of.

Choose one of your passions and do some research on it. Find information that other people have put together to help you understand your passion better and ways to pursue it.

We don't have to do everything from scratch. We can learn from other people's research and experiences.

Activity Thirty-One: Call a Friend

We've seen now that it's important to share with others and the value that it can have.

Call a friend and invite them for a chat. Share your main source of inspiration with them and tell them why it's important to you. Ask them about theirs and what they do when inspiration is lacking.

Sharing these kinds of details not only helps us to reflect on them but also helps us to build a better relationship with those who are closest to us.

SEEK YOUR TRIBE

A tribe, or community, is a group of people that share the same interest in something. A close community, and one that we should all want to be a part of, is one where the members care for each other, trust one another, and have a connection deeper than just being acquaintances.

Being part of a community can help to make us feel like we belong somewhere and that someone cares. We can lead a more fulfilling life. Some of the benefits of being part of a community include:

- **Growth:** When you are part of a community, you learn from those around you and receive constructive feedback on your own progress. This can really help to accelerate growth in your passions and skills.

- **Joy:** When we socialize with others and relate to them on a personal level, this alleviates stress and makes us feel joyful.
- **Support network:** A community is an automatic support network as soon as you join one. To lead a meaningful life, we need a support network around us.
- **Improved communication skills:** A community provides a safe space to communicate with others and cultivate your communication skills.
- **Purpose:** When we feel like we belong, we also feel like we have a purpose. A community helps us with both.

Ready to join a community? It's easier than you think. There are both online and physical communities, and which one is best for you would depend on your reason for joining the community. Some hobbies are best when shared in person, while others can be done virtually.

For offline communities, you can start by researching whether any communities in your area pique your interest (i.e., a community that aligns with your interests and passions). For online, you can just research ones related to your passions. They don't have to be in your area. Search on platforms like Medium, LinkedIn, Reddit, or Facebook.

When looking into a community, whether online or offline, make sure you look at what they stand for, what the purpose of the community is, how many members are part of the community, how active they are, any rules they may have, and whether there are any requirements or costs for joining the community.

Once you join the community, remember to introduce yourself, tell them how you found them, why you're excited to network with them, and why you are passionate about the community's vision.

Activity Thirty-Two: Online Forums

Online forums and social media groups are great ways to connect instantly with a community. They are generally very welcoming, and you can learn a lot from them.

Search for two online forums or social media groups related to your interest and join them. You can ask an adult or friend to help you look if you're not sure. Remember to practice good internet etiquette and stay safe.

Connecting online with people with the same interest as you are bound to motivate and inspire you to take your interest even further. You will see a big difference in how you approach this once you're part of something bigger—trust me.

Activity Thirty-Three: Get Involved

One of the best ways to join a community and find your place in the community is to get involved.

Look for any community event or webinar that will be hosted in the near future (related to your interests or passion) and find out how you can get involved. It doesn't matter how small your involvement is; the more you put up your hand, the bigger your role will become. Trust the process and start small.

This is an excellent way to get your name out there and socialize with the other people in the community on a different level. The more you can interact with them, the better.

Activity Thirty-Four: Talk to Someone

When we share our experiences or learnings, we are also learning from them. It allows us to reflect and receive feedback.

Find someone that you can talk to about the community you've joined and share a tip or trick you learned from the community with them. Have a discussion about how the community has influenced and helped you.

Not only do you get to reflect on what you've learned, but you might even inspire the other person to join a community as well.

THE POWER OF PASSION PROJECTS

You are going to love this one!

Maybe you've heard of a passion project before but never really understood what it meant. Or maybe you know, but you haven't had the time. Or maybe you've never heard of it. It doesn't matter which category you fall into; it's definitely time to take on a passion project.

A passion project is a project that you decide to start or take on because you have a special interest or are curious about something specific. No one really drives it on your behalf—you decide how quickly the project progresses and when it's finished. In general, it's also not tied to any academic or professional requirements and is purely for personal gain. It's a very fulfilling experience because it taps into everything important to you.

Some benefits of starting a passion project include showcasing your skills, showing that you can commit to something, cultivating self-satisfaction, demonstrating that you are self-disciplined, and working on skill-building; it also helps you to explore your interests.

I'm sure you've heard me say this a few times about various things, but starting is the hardest part. Once you can get the ball rolling, you just need to keep up the momentum. I've outlined some tips below to help you get started once you get to the activities.

- When deciding on the topic for your passion project, make sure that it's something you want to pursue in the long term. It has to be something that you are very passionate about. Otherwise, it will feel like work, and you will struggle to keep it going.
- If you need any help or support, ask! Reach out to your parents, friends, or even your community for help. You don't have to do all of it by yourself. A passion project is something you put in motion and drive from your end, but it doesn't have to be a one-man show.
- Pace yourself. Don't try and do everything in a day or a week. Set realistic and achievable goals (we're exploring SMART goals in the next chapter) and work toward them. A passion project is a marathon, not a sprint.

- Make time to spend on your passion project. It's great to get an idea going, but it's equally as important to then put in the work. When you choose something you really enjoy, finding the time shouldn't be that difficult.
- Be kind and patient with yourself. It's not going to become a success overnight, and it may seem like it's failing before it starts getting better. Be patient. Identify when there are issues, and find ways to adapt the plan.

Activity Thirty-Five: Get Thinking

The very first step to starting a passion project is to brainstorm some ideas. Remember the tips above when you do this.

Maybe you're not sure where to start. This activity is to help with exactly that. Get your pen and paper ready to scribble down a few ideas of what your passion project can be about. Some things to consider when you're brainstorming:

- Use your skills and talents: We've explored this a bit already. Make sure that you keep them in mind during the brainstorming. Try to utilize them as much as possible.
- Remember your interests: You've already done the work to find out what your interests are. Make sure that you combine them with what you're passionate about.
- Find a need: Do some research to see whether there is a need in the community that you can help fill with your

passion project. It might help you to get started with an idea.

Some ideas you can look at include writing a book on something you're passionate about, starting a blog on the topic, developing a mobile app, or even having a fundraiser in the community. Deciding how to translate your passion into a project is the hardest part, but with the above guidelines and the internet at your disposal, I have no doubt that you will find something!

Activity Thirty-Six: Do Some Planning and Start

Now for further planning and actually kicking off with the project. You can do this! It's time to narrow down all the ideas you came up with in the previous activity to only one.

Once you have a clear idea of what you want to do, it's time to put everything in place and change the world one passion project at a time. The first thing you want to do is note down any investment you need to make, resources you'll need, or support you require to deliver the project for the ideal outcome. Make sure to also list what the minimum investment that will be required is and any alternatives that can also make it work. Think about any issues you might experience to put measures in place to manage or avoid them.

Remember to start small. You don't have to dedicate all your time to your passion project. If you don't have more than an hour a day or week, don't neglect other responsibilities. The deeper you get into the project, the easier it will be to find time to spend on it.

Activity Thirty-Seven: Reflection

This activity can only be done after you've started with your passion project.

Reflect on your experience to date and what you've learned after completing or making progress on your passion project. If you have only done the planning and just kicked off, that's okay too. Write down anything you've learned about yourself, the community, or any lessons so far.

Reflection really is one of the most powerful tools we can use to help us grow continuously and exponentially. It helps us to connect with our inner selves and identify weak points.

CHAPTER 4 SUMMARY

- Getting creative is about more than just drawing or painting. There are many ways we can get creative and improve our mental health in the process.
- Being creative can help us find new things we are interested in and start new hobbies. Having a hobby is an essential part of leading a fulfilling life.
- A hobby should be fun and build us up. We don't always have to be good at it; we just need to enjoy it.
- A lack of inspiration can cause us to shy away from creativity and pursuing our hobbies. We can find

inspiration in everyday things like taking a walk, reading a book, or even visiting a museum.

- Joining a community is another great way to tap into our interests and pursue our hobbies in a more structured way. Online and offline communities are great!
- We choose to pursue a passion project without any academic or professional drive to do it. However, we can definitely gain a lot from it. A passion project should be something we are passionate about and enjoy to ensure we don't give up halfway.

Are you ready to get into practical goal setting? The next chapter is all about how to set goals and how to keep the momentum going, especially when it becomes problematic.

TURNING DREAMS INTO GOALS

In this chapter, we are going to discuss goal-setting in more detail and how to move from planning to action. This will help you to transform your dreams and passions into achievable goals. You can make significant progress toward what you want in life through effective planning and tracking.

Let's compare two young adults: Tony, who wants to be a musician and has clear goals and an action plan to reach his dreams, and Therese, who has a dream but doesn't actively work toward it.

Tony has known since he was very young that he wants to pursue a music career. His dream is to be a famous singer, guitarist, and songwriter by the time he's 30. His whole life revolves around the incremental goals he has set for himself, and he rarely deviates from his action plan. He has been invited to perform at a few local pubs and even has a regular spot where everyone knows and loves him.

Therese wants to be a photography model for big brands in fashion. When they were younger, they participated in a few local pageants but haven't done anything since. They have no experience with being professionally photographed and hope that someone will see their potential one day when they're sitting in the park. They don't have a concrete action plan or any goals on how to fulfill their dream other than the hope that a photographer will notice their unique beauty.

Setting goals and developing an action plan to work toward them are imperative for long-term motivation and determination. We briefly mentioned the Goal Setting Theory in Chapter 1. There are five guidelines to the Goal Setting Theory:

- **Clarity:** There must be a clear vision of exactly what you want to achieve. A lack of clarity will result in setting goals that are not achievable, which may result in reduced motivation. Clarity is a key component of goal setting. We will explore this more in Chapter 5.
- **Committed action:** Committing to achieving your goal is the next step. Just having a plan with no action steps will reduce your chances of being successful.
- **Support system:** A support system consists of people who are there to support you in achieving your goal. They help to keep you accountable and provide additional support you may need during the journey. This is a pivotal part of achieving your goals.
- **Progress over perfection:** Focusing on progress instead of perfection can make a big difference in whether or not you achieve your goal. Here it's

important to break the goal into smaller pieces and celebrate the small wins instead of striving to perfectly complete the goal in one try.

- **Flexibility:** Having an open mind is significant. Sometimes, your circumstances might change, and you may need to adapt your goal to fit the new circumstances. It's pointless trying to achieve something that may no longer be relevant. This is also why you should constantly revise your goal and make sure you're still chasing the right thing.

MASTERING GOAL SETTING

Setting goals can be a difficult task, especially when you're not sure how to do it. Luckily, there are many models out there that you can use to help you. The method we will discuss in this book is SMART goal-setting. You may have heard about it already, but in case you haven't, I have covered the basics below. SMART goals are:

- **Specific:** It's important to be specific when setting a goal. The more specific you are, the better. Vague goals make it difficult for us to work toward them.
- **Measurable:** Being able to measure how you are tracking toward your goal and how far you are from achieving it is very important.
- **Attainable:** Your goal should be attainable. It shouldn't be something that is out of reach. In saying that, you shouldn't be scared to stretch yourself.

- **Relevant:** You should set a goal that makes sense and is relevant to your journey. It should align with your future vision and values.
- **Time-based:** A goal without a time component is very difficult to reach. You should set a reasonable timeframe for achieving the goal.

Let's look at a quick example that demonstrates why SMART goals are so powerful. A vague goal might look something like this:

I want to save money.

Although that's a great goal to have, it's not specific. Because it's not specific, it's definitely not measurable, which also makes it hard to decide whether it's attainable. It's too vague to really work toward. Let's use the same goal and make it a SMART goal:

I want to save $5,000 in the next 12 months so that I can take a trip to Paris for fashion week.

Let's break it down in the SMART goal. *Is it*:

- *specific?* Yes, I know exactly how much I want to save and why.
- *measurable?* Yes, I can easily track my progress.
- *attainable?* Yes, I can break the SMART goal into smaller goals and save a little bit each month.
- *relevant?* Yes, I am very interested in fashion, and going to Paris for fashion week is a dream come true.
- *time-based?* Yes, I have 12 months to do it.

Activity Thirty-Eight: Formulate a SMART Goal

By setting goals, we know exactly what we are working toward and how long it will take to get there, and we have something to look forward to. Goal-setting is a very important aspect of personal growth and development.

Grab a pen and paper and write down one SMART goal related to your passion or interest. Use the SMART acronym to ensure that your goal meets the requirements of a SMART goal.

Be very intentional and specific. You can even link it to your passion project. Using the SMART method will help to set goals that are easier to chase after.

Activity Thirty-Nine: Share Your Goal

You know the saying by now: Sharing is caring.

Share the SMART goal that you have set with a friend or family member and ask for their thoughts. This will also help to keep you accountable for the commitment that you've made.

Having someone that keeps you accountable is so powerful. It's not easy to always be disciplined, but having someone support you and cheer you on makes it a lot easier.

Activity Forty: Goal Reflection

It's time to go back in time again to learn from our mistakes and see how we can do better in the future.

Think back to a goal that you set for yourself before that you didn't achieve. Write it down and identify what went wrong. Was the goal a SMART goal? Which parts of the SMART goal did you miss when setting the goal? How can you rewrite the goal to make it a SMART goal?

By looking at a past experience and applying a new lens to it, we can easily identify what went wrong and how we can prevent those same mistakes in future goals. The point is not to make you feel like you could have done better back then but rather that you are better equipped now to succeed.

BREAKING BIG GOALS INTO BITS

Some goals can seem a little intimidating when they're big or long-term goals. Maybe you don't know where to even start. This is where chunking, or breaking up goals, comes into play. The best thing you can do is to break your one big SMART goal into smaller, more manageable goals.

When we break down our goals into smaller goals, we are less likely to procrastinate. Procrastination mostly stems from not knowing where to start or feeling like we're not making any progress. The smaller goals help us to keep momentum going because we're constantly chasing something new. We are also more likely to get the details right because we're focused on the smaller things instead of an overarching goal that we're trying to reach.

Here are a few simple steps that you can follow to break down your goal into smaller goals:

- Once you have clearly defined your goal, write down exactly what is necessary for you to achieve it. This can be at a high level; you will drill down into the details later. This may include things like doing research, networking with people, finding a part-time job, enrolling in a course, and so on.
- Next, you want to take the above information and divide your goal into a few high-level subgoals.
- When you have the subgoals defined and in order, take the first one and determine a few actionable steps that you can take to reach it. The smaller, the better.
- All you need to do now is start with the first small action that needs to be completed. Pick a date that you want to start, execute it, rinse, and repeat until you achieve your big goal.
- Don't be afraid to make adjustments along the way, where needed. Sometimes our vision changes while we're going through the process, and that's okay. It doesn't mean you have to start from scratch—you can adapt your current goals to align with the new vision.

Let's look at a quick example: cooking a meal. Just starting with "I want to cook pasta this Saturday for my family" can be quite intimidating for someone who hasn't cooked before. Instead of keeping it as a big goal, let's break it down into a few bite-sized subgoals:

- I need to find a recipe for the meal that I want to cook.
- I need to ensure that I have all the equipment needed to make the meal.
- I need to look at the recipe and identify any cooking skills I need to research.
- I need to research the necessary skills (if any).
- I should look at the list of ingredients and identify whether I need to get anything from the shop.
- I need to go to the shop to purchase any ingredients that I may need.
- I should read the recipe and prepare the ingredients before I start cooking.
- I need to follow the recipe to make the meal.

By breaking one big goal into a few subgoals, you can focus on one thing at a time. There is no need to worry about cooking the ingredients when you are still preparing them. We can reach our goals one bite at a time.

Activity Forty-One: Breaking Down SMART Goals

Use your SMART goal from Activity Thirty-Eight and break it down into smaller, easily attainable goals. If the SMART goal is not big enough to break down even more, formulate a new one that you can use. Remember to refer to the tips in the previous section for help.

When we break it down into smaller steps, it's easier to make progress because we can see that we are getting closer to achieving our goal. It becomes less overwhelming and encourages steady progress.

CREATE YOUR ACTION PLAN

When we set goals but have no plan in place, they just become dreams. Without an action plan, achieving our goals becomes difficult.

An action plan helps you to commit to the goal and keep momentum. It's a detailed plan about when you're planning on working on your goal, for how long, and how long it will take. It helps to keep you on track and slowly work toward success.

We have already covered the first two steps to creating an action plan, which is to set a SMART goal and identify tasks that need to be performed. Now it's time to allocate resources that you might need per task to be performed. Knowing what resources are required will help to prevent blockers later on. Resources could be additional people you need, money, equipment, or anything else to help you achieve your goal.

Your SMART goal should already have a timeframe, but the smaller goals and tasks may not. It's time to set some deadlines to ensure that you stay on track to accomplishing your SMART goal within the time you settled on. Be specific when setting the deadlines and identifying milestones. You can use various tools to help with this, including mobile or online apps and even planners where you can physically make notes.

The only thing you need to do now is monitor the progress using your action plan and make any adjustments if necessary.

Keep a close eye on the milestones and revise the timeline sooner rather than later, if required.

Activity Forty-Two: Create an Action Plan

Using the steps above, grab a pen and paper or download a mobile app and create an action plan for your SMART goal and subgoals from Activity Thirty-Eight and Activity Forty-One.

While creating the action plan, identify potential hurdles that you might experience and brainstorm solutions. Review your action plan with a trusted friend or family member who may have some suggestions on how you can improve it and make any necessary adjustments.

Keep checking your action plan and goals and ensure that they still align with your vision. Don't be afraid to make adjustments.

KEEP TABS AND CELEBRATE

Just setting goals and working toward them is not enough. We must track the progress we're making. By doing so, we:

- ensure that we remain accountable for what we've committed to achieve.
- can identify any roadblocks that may exist and come up with solutions before it's too late.
- prioritize the most important tasks and those that might take longer to complete than others.

- can easily measure the progress we're making toward our goal and know exactly how far we are from reaching it.
- make adjustments early on, where necessary.

Above all else, by tracking our progress, we stay motivated throughout. It's easier to keep pushing when it's clear what has already been done and how close we are to achieving what we want to achieve. It may be challenging to track progress when we're not sure how to do it or have the right tools to do it. Luckily, there are many tools, online and offline, that we can utilize to complete the job. I have listed a few below:

- **Bullet journaling:** This is such a fun and creative way to track goals! It's a blank canvas, and you decide how you want to do it. It's old school with pen and paper, but if you're even a little artsy, you'll love it. Check out a few ideas online, especially sites like Pinterest.
- **Old-fashioned to-do list:** You can go really old school and just create a list with checkboxes where you check it off when you've completed a task. Quick, easy, hassle-free.
- **Fun charts:** Why not try to write the subgoals and steps in chart form and use funky stickers to tick off when a goal or step has been completed? It might sound boring, but think of all the options when it comes to stickers...
- **Whiteboard method:** You can also use a large whiteboard where you can add and remove things easily. You can personalize it using different colored markers, sticky notes, and magnets.

- **Gamify:** Make a game out of it. There is this great app called Kanban that you can download. You need to create an account, but once it's set up, it's really such a great app to use. You get a tree, set goals, and track them. The more steps you complete and the closer you get to achieving your goal, the more the tree grows.
- **Trello:** This is a mobile and desktop app that you can use to track your goals. It's highly personalized and great for first-time users.

The last thing to remember about goal setting is that you need to celebrate the small wins. Although for some, just reaching the milestones will be enough, most of us need a little more help in the form of rewards. It doesn't matter how you decide to do it, as long as you take some time to celebrate what you've achieved. Be intentional with when you celebrate. For example, you don't want to celebrate every single day because then it might get boring very quickly. Keep the celebrating (and rewarding) for milestones that have been reached, but make sure that they are also often enough so that you don't lose momentum.

Knowing that there is a reward waiting for you helps with that extra bit of motivation to keep pushing. Rewards can be small, like going out for an ice cream or a movie. For bigger milestones, you can go bigger. Make sure that the reward makes sense for the goal or milestone you've achieved.

Activity Forty-Three: Track Your Progress

There are many goal-tracking methods, certainly more than what I have listed here.

Take a look at the list of tracking methods or find one that you like and implement it with your SMART goal. Make sure that you choose one that you know you will diligently stick to, and that will get you excited about making progress.

Choosing the right tracking tool can make a big difference in how fast you make progress in your journey. Try out a few if you're not sure which one to choose.

Activity Forty-Four: Celebrate the Small Wins

How you choose to celebrate doesn't matter.

Once you've reached a milestone, take some time out and celebrate the win. In fact, just getting this far in with your goal setting and tracking deserves a celebration! Treat yourself in a small but meaningful way. You know what makes you tick and what motivates you.

Celebrating a small win will help to solidify the process and motivate you to keep going, so don't skip it!

Activity Forty-Five: Make Adjustments

Sometimes, we over- or underestimate something, and that's okay.

Review your tracking data at the end of the week and decide whether the timeline and goals you've set all make sense. If needed, make a few adjustments to the plan.

The last thing you want to happen is to run out of time for a goal you set yourself or even get bored waiting for a new challenge. Making adjustments as you go is as important as creating an action plan in the first place.

CHAPTER 5 SUMMARY

- When setting goals, the SMART goal methodology is very useful. Goals must be specific, measurable, attainable, relevant, and time-based.
- When a goal seems too big, and you don't know where to start, breaking it up into subgoals can help.
- Having goals is great, but along with them, we need an action plan to help us execute them.
- Tracking progress toward goals and celebrating the small wins is an essential step to achieving our goals.

Now that you're a master at setting and tracking goals, are you ready to work on time management? It's something many of us struggle with because we never seem to have time for everything.

The next chapter will equip you with effective time management skills. By learning how to organize and prioritize your tasks, you can create a balanced life and achieve your goals.

MASTERING TIME MANAGEMENT

Effective time management is a crucial skill, but very few have mastered it. We are often so inundated with tasks and to-do lists that it feels like there are never enough hours in the day to do it all. However, some people manage just fine and have the same hours in the day and, most of the time, more tasks to complete.

Time management means deciding how to spend your time and dividing it between the various activities or tasks you need to perform. It helps us to work smarter, not harder.

Let's compare Patricia and Chris.

Patricia excels in every aspect of her life. She makes time for school, her social life, and free time, and she even has a part-time job to help her reach her goals. She knows what is and isn't important and makes sure to prioritize the tasks accordingly.

She doesn't allow anything to steal her time and leads a fulfilling life.

Chris has very poor time management skills. He was never taught how to prioritize or manage his time effectively, which has led to many missed opportunities and debilitating anxiety. Because of the anxiety, he really struggles to do anything during the day and ends up doing nothing on most days. It feels empty and meaningless, living the same day over and over.

Which one are you? If you relate to Chris in this scenario, that's okay. This chapter is full of great tips to get you on the right track.

BALANCE BETWEEN BOOKS AND LIFE

To really feel fulfilled and happy, we need to strike a balance between academic pursuits, social activities, and personal activities. Focusing on one area more than the others can lead to unhappiness and the feeling that something is missing. It can also cause stress and make you feel overwhelmed.

This is why it's so important to make time for everything, especially unwinding and recharging your social battery. A balanced life can lead to overall well-being and success.

Making time for everything is definitely part of time management, which is why it's an important aspect to cover when it comes to cultivating a motivational mindset. Motivation definitely decreases when we start feeling overwhelmed.

TIME TRICKS FOR TEENS

There are quite a few tried and tested techniques that you can use to manage your time effectively. I have listed a few of them below, including some tips that should help you.

- **The Eisenhower matrix:** We'll look at this method in the next section for How to Prioritize and Stay Sorted, but it's a great trick to use for time management.
- **Set deadlines:** Even if you don't need to have a deadline, set one for yourself. This will make sure that you prioritize the right tasks and not accumulate a bunch of tasks that you carry over every single day.
- **Eat the frog:** That sounds terrible and definitely does not refer to a real frog, but it encourages you to do the thing you want to do the least first. Most of the time, the task that we keep putting off is the task that is making us procrastinate the most and lose precious time.
- **The Pomodoro Technique:** You might have used this technique before without even knowing it. The goal is to get yourself to focus on a specific task for a set amount of time and then take a break for a set amount of time, repeating the process until you've done what you need to do. The general rule of thumb is to focus for 25 minutes, take a five-minute break, and then focus again for 25 minutes. Once you reach 100 minutes, you should ideally increase the break to 15 or 20 minutes.
- **Have a plan for the day:** When we don't have a plan, we tend to waste time instead of spending our time on

something useful. By planning out your day, you are more likely to be productive and get more done so that you have less to do tomorrow. You can use a calendar or daily planner to do this.

- **Identify when you are most productive:** While you're planning your day, try to identify when you are most effective and plan your tasks around that. For example, I know that my productivity dwindles just after lunchtime, so I try to get the most critical and time-consuming tasks done early in the morning.

You can use these techniques for home life, school, university, or even your work life once you start your first job. Once you understand the method, it's easy to apply it in various situations.

Maybe you're wondering why time management is even essential. The benefits of effective time management are multifaceted. It teaches us how to prioritize effectively, how to make valuable decisions, reduce stress, lessen distractions, increase free time, and improve academic performance.

Activity Forty-Six: Pick a Time-Management Technique

I'm sure you knew this was coming by now.

I want you to pick one of the time management techniques and use it when doing your homework. Choose just one, and afterward, reflect on how the technique helped you or didn't. If it wasn't that successful, try another one tomorrow. Chat with a friend and ask them what time management technique they use. Share your experiences, and maybe try theirs out, too.

HOW TO PRIORITIZE AND STAY SORTED

To prioritize something means to accurately rank it in the level of importance, making sure that the most critical tasks are completed first. This is directly related to being organized because being organized involves arranging tasks or items in a structured way. The more organized we are, the better our prioritization skills are, and the more effectively we will manage our time.

There are various methods to prioritize tasks. Choose one that works for you and stick to it. You might need to get acquainted with more than one method because you can't always use all of them in all situations. I have listed some of the ones I've used below. For all of them, you will need to make a list of all the tasks that need to be completed, like a to-do list. This is the easy part. Once you have your list, you need to assign priority to the tasks. This is where the methods come in.

- **The Eisenhower matrix:** consists of four boxes. Every task that needs to be completed can fit into one of the four boxes.

Important and not urgent	Important and urgent
Not urgent and not important	Urgent and not important

- ○ Something important but not urgent can be postponed and assigned second priority after the urgent and essential tasks.
- ○ Something important and urgent should be prioritized over everything else.
- ○ Something not urgent and not necessary can be removed from your list completely. Why waste time on something that is not urgent and also not important to do?
- ○ Something urgent but not important can actually be given to someone else to do if that is a possibility for you.

- **Impact effort matrix:** This matrix also consists of four boxes, like the Eisenhower matrix, but it uses a different methodology for grouping tasks.

High-effort and low-impact	High-effort and high-impact
Low-effort and low-impact	Low-effort and high-impact

- ○ After you have allocated each task to a quadrant, you want to start with the low-effort and high-impact tasks, followed by the high-effort and high-impact tasks. This will ensure that you get the ones done that will make the biggest difference.

- **The ABCDE method:** To use this method, you need to note down all the tasks that you need to complete for the day and then assign one of the letters to it (A, B, C, D, or E). You then complete them in that order.

- A is for tasks that are very important and that must be done as soon as possible.
- B is for tasks that should be done, but they don't have to be done right away.
- C is for tasks that are nice to do. Those things that are on your list that you enjoy doing but are not that important.
- D is for anything that you can delegate to someone else to do.
- E is for tasks that you can remove from your list.

- **Bubble sort method:** With this method, you compare two tasks to each other and decide which one is more important than the other one. It's best to look at these tasks side-by-side to compare. This works best on something like sticky notes that you can easily move around.

  - Write all the tasks that need to be completed on sticky notes, one sticky note per task. For the explanation, we will just call them Task 1 up until Task 4, but on your sticky note, you will have the actual task.
  - Arrange them all side-by-side and compare Task 1 and Task 2. Which one is more important to complete?
  - If it's Task 2, you move it to the beginning of the

line and then compare the next two, i.e., Task 1
and Task 3.

- o   If Task 3 is then more important, you will need to
  compare Task 2 (the one that was moved to the
  beginning) and Task 3 with each other to see
  which one is more important.
- o   Whenever a new combination exists, you will
  need to compare them again to ensure you get
  the right priority.
- o   Once you've gone through all of them, you should
  have a good idea of which ones are most
  important to complete.

Activity Forty-Seven: Create a To-Do List

Creating a to-do list is the first step in ensuring things get done. Without a to-do list, how do you remember what you need to accomplish for the day?

Create a to-do list for the week and prioritize your tasks accordingly. You can use any of the methods above or your own prioritization method. As you complete tasks, check them off your to-do list and adjust the list as needed. At the end of the week, review what you've accomplished and what you could do to improve next time.

Organizing and prioritizing tasks is the most effective way to ensure things get done. Don't assume that you will remember or that you will get to everything eventually.

Together with your to-do list, create a weekly schedule where you make time to also focus on the other areas of your life where you might not have an active task, like taking some time to watch your favorite series as a personal activity or catching up with a friend over coffee to refill your social meter.

TACKLING TIME-WASTERS

We have to address the white elephant in the room: time-wasters. We live in a world where it's all around us, all the time. It's easy to get trapped in the endless TikTok or Instagram rabbit hole or even binge-watching an original Netflix series. I'm not saying that you shouldn't be indulging at all, but most of the time, these time-wasters eat up all of our time, and we even postpone essential tasks just to keep at it.

I'm sure we've all been there. It's almost time for bed, so instead of getting into something important, we choose to scroll TikTok for a few minutes. Before we know it, we've gone so deep into the rabbit hole that it is five hours later and way past the time we planned to go to bed.

While some downtime is necessary, we can manage it better to ensure that we don't end up wasting hours of our day. Let's look at some tips that can help you make time for it without allowing it to rule the day:

- Have set times for social media breaks during the day, and don't allow yourself to open any social media sites outside of those times. Since they will be dedicated timeslots, you probably won't be doing anything else anyway, so it should give you enough time to scroll to your heart's content. Set an alarm when the timeslot is over and be disciplined enough to put social media aside once it's over. This also goes for watching television.

- Don't try to multitask. We actually can't multitask. Our brains don't have the capacity to fully focus on more than one thing at a time. When we do two or three things at the same time, our focus constantly jumps from one thing to the next, meaning that we never give our full attention to one task. This could lead to a delay in getting things done.
- Stop procrastinating. The daily planner and to-do list should help you with this, but there is no guarantee. The thing with procrastination is we always find something else we would rather do. Add them to your to-do list so that you have no excuse to actually procrastinate.
- Make sure that the tasks that you need to complete are clear and that there is no ambiguity. Sometimes we procrastinate or waste time because we're not sure what we're actually supposed to be doing.

Once you start managing these time-wasters, you'll find that you have a lot more free time on your hands to do other things that you enjoy that enrich your life.

Activity Forty-Eight: Identify Your Time-Wasters

So, let's put what we just learned into practice.

Think about the typical time-wasters in your life and make a list of the top three. Set some goals on how you plan to reduce them, such as scheduling specific time for television, deactivating your social media accounts, or even locking away your phone for the lion's share of the day.

Implement at least one strategy to manage your top three time-wasters for a week. After the week is over, reflect on the difference it made to your day, note your stress levels, and see how much more free time you had. If you think you can do it differently for the next week, try a new strategy.

CHAPTER 6 SUMMARY

- It's important to live a well-balanced life by making time for school, family, friends, and yourself.
- There are many time management techniques that are worth checking out, such as setting deadlines, eating the frog, the Pomodoro technique, planning your day, and knowing when you are most productive.
- Prioritizing has everything to do with time management. Some ways you can prioritize tasks include the Eisenhower matrix, the impact effort matrix, the ABCDE method, and the bubble sort method.

- To ensure that you manage your time well, you also need to get rid of or manage any time-wasters in your daily life.

You will use time management skills your entire life. The quicker you become a master at it, the better. You really will be happier once you learn how to manage your time well.

For the next chapter, we're going to have a closer look at building positive habits and a positive mindset. The contents of the chapter will help you understand the power of a positive perspective and habits in shaping your life. You can boost your mental well-being and productivity by adopting gratitude and daily routines.

BUILDING POSITIVE HABITS AND MINDSET

Having a positive mindset is more than just trying to always be positive. It does start with positive thinking and embracing the good with gratitude. We will look at positive thinking, gratitude's role, why a daily routine is essential, and how to beat procrastination.

Before we get into it, let's compare two teens: Alex and Anna.

Alex has discovered the power of gratitude and practices it daily. They always have their positive thinking hat on and look for solutions instead of focusing on problems. This means that they are happier overall and feel fulfilled by the end of the day. They have a daily routine that works, leading to more productive days.

Anna struggles to get out of her negative thinking patterns and procrastinates a lot. This leads to her missing out on multiple opportunities and steals her joy every day. Because of this, she prefers to distance herself from others and only has a select few people she talks to.

When we start embracing gratitude and positive thinking, our whole life changes. Why not give it a try?

THE MAGIC OF THINKING POSITIVE

What does it mean to embrace positive thinking? What is positive thinking, is it possible to influence our thoughts in that way, and why is positive thinking important? Let's take a closer look at it.

Positive thinking is not necessarily always experiencing positive emotions or even behaviors. Embracing positive thinking doesn't mean we can improve our overall mental health and well-being by leaning into positive thinking instead of negative thinking. It's connected to your thoughts. It's the ability to always see the positive in a situation and to turn any negative thoughts into positive ones.

There are so many benefits to positive thinking, including a better immune system, reduced chances of developing anxiety and depression, better coping skills, and improved stress management. People who embrace positive thinking even live longer (Cherry, 2023b).

Activity Forty-Nine: Identifying Negative Thoughts

We need to be able to identify a negative thought as soon as we have it and have the ability to reframe it. The reframed thought should still be true and must be helpful. We spoke about positive self-talk in Chapter 3, and this activity can relate quite a bit to Activity Sixteen.

Identify three negative thoughts you often have and reframe them into positive ones. The first step is to know that it is a negative thought, question whether the thought is accurate, and then replace it with something more helpful that is also true. For example, if the negative thought is "I'm not good enough," you can't replace it with "I'm incredible because I've won a Nobel prize" if that's not true. You can replace it with "I have been created to be incredible, and I am good enough."

Activity Fifty: Start With Positivity

The way you start your day sets the tone of how your day will go. When you start it on a positive note, things can only get better!

For one week, I want you to start each day with a positive affirmation. Make sure that you say it out loud. Even better if you can do it in the mirror. I know that it might feel awkward in the beginning, but there's a reason why so many people do it in the mirror. It makes a difference.

It can be short and simple. It doesn't have to be a whole paragraph. A short sentence is enough. Here are some examples to inspire you:

- I am deeply loved and highly favored just the way I am.
- I can conquer anything that comes my way.

- Today is going to be a good day.
- Today, I choose myself.
- Every day is a blessing.
- I am worthy of love and affection.

At the end of the week, reflect on any changes in your mood or general outlook.

THE ROLE OF GRATITUDE IN LIFE

I'm sure you've heard about gratitude. Maybe you've even read the third book in *You Are Your Mindset* series called *A Gratitude Mindset for Teens*. If you haven't, you can find it on Amazon!

Gratitude isn't just about saying thank you. It's about genuinely being grateful for everything you have and realizing that your life is worth more than the problems you might face. Practicing gratitude helps us to focus on the good and creates a positive outlook on life. There is generally also an action related to the feeling of gratitude, like doing something in return.

There are many ways we can practice gratitude, such as keeping a gratitude journal, expressing gratitude toward someone, or even using meditation to help focus on gratitude.

Practicing gratitude has many benefits, such as:

- cultivating and maintaining healthy relationships.
- reduced blood pressure, anxiety, and depression.
- improved sleep.
- a better self-esteem.

Activity Fifty-One: Make a Gratitude List

Writing down the things we are grateful for is an excellent way to remind ourselves of the good that surrounds us.

Every day for a week, make a list of three things that you are grateful for that day. Try not to repeat any of them and see how many unique things you can find. You can even build this into dinnertime with the family. Challenge each person to list three things they are grateful for that day while you are all sitting down for dinner.

Something magical happens when we start recognizing the good things in our lives. It changes our whole mindset, and we start focusing on the good instead of the bad.

Activity Fifty-Two: Express Gratitude

Everyone loves hearing that they are appreciated for the little things they do. We rarely express sincere gratitude to those around us and should do it more.

For this activity, I want you to choose someone who has impacted your life (big or small) and express gratitude for what they've done. You can do this in person, through an old-school letter, or even with a text message. The method doesn't matter. It's about the message.

By expressing gratitude to those who make a difference, we build a stronger bond with them and let them know they are valued. There's nothing better than knowing someone is grateful you exist.

Now that you've practiced some gratitude, reflect on how this has impacted your daily life and well-being.

DAILY ROUTINES FOR WINNING DAYS

I know that having a routine might sound boring and like a lot of work, but our brains actually like routine. They like knowing what to expect and what should happen next. A daily routine can be the difference between achieving your goals and missing the mark.

We all have some form of daily routine that works for us—for example, a morning routine of getting ready. My typical morning routine is to get up, make coffee, drink my coffee in peace, brush my teeth, do my facial routine (which is a routine all on its own), get dressed, do my hair and make-up, and then leave the house. Some mornings, I will squeeze in a quick gym session if I know I can't do it in the evening. It's a good routine, and it makes me more efficient. When there is a small deviation in it, my whole day seems to be upside down.

Having a structured day has many benefits, including better time management, increased productivity, no need to plan more, breaking bad habits and creating good ones, reducing procrastination, and many more.

Activity Fifty-Three: Morning Routine

I've shared my morning routine with you. Now, it's time to create your own.

Write down a simple morning routine that you can follow for a week. Try to incorporate some of the activities we've done, such as gratitude and mindfulness. Track how well you stick to it and make any adjustments where needed. Perhaps you wake up too late or spend more time doing something specific, which pushes out all the other tasks. After you have followed it for a week, reflect on how the new routine has affected your day.

BEAT PROCRASTINATION AND DISTRACTIONS

Procrastination is the thief of time. It might give us the illusion that we have enough time to do what we need to do, but in reality, it just steals all our time and causes excessive anxiety once we realize that we've procrastinated too long. The danger of procrastination is putting things out and eventually not getting to it because it's like a cycle. We procrastinate, we feel anxious about it, our mental health takes a beating, and we procrastinate even more because of it.

There are many reasons why you might be in the procrastination cycle. Some of the reasons may include self-doubt (not believing that you will do a good job), anger (toward authority, i.e., wanting to show your parents that you do things on your own terms), and perfectionism (always wanting everything to be perfect so delaying it because you know the work you need to do to make sure it's perfect). But it could also be a very obvious one, like just not wanting to deal with something at that moment so you choose to do something else (hopefully productive) instead or being distracted by your environment.

Whatever the reason is, it's important to get a hold of it earlier in life and know how to deal with it now. Here are some tips to help you:

- **Break it up:** Perhaps you're procrastinating because it feels like the task is just too big, and you don't know where to start. Just like goals, you can break a big task up into manageable pieces and plan when you're going to do what.
- **Be motivated and inspired:** The more motivated and inspired we are, the easier it will be to do what we need to do. Refer back to Chapter 4 if you need a refresher on this.
- **Just do it:** I know this sounds pretty easy, but when it comes down to it, it's challenging. I would suggest you set a time in the day when you will focus on the task specifically and make sure you keep yourself to it. Once you get started, you might realize that you made a big deal out of it for nothing or realize that it's going to take some time, and the initial start will act as motivation to set the next steps. I've said it before, and I'll repeat it: Getting started is the hardest part.
- **Be organized:** Use some of the time-management techniques to help you become more organized and plan your days. Stick to the schedule as much as you can.

- **Remove distractions:** Sometimes, it's the environment you are in that leads to you procrastinating. For example, if you have a television in your room, it might make it a lot more difficult to study because you'll be tempted to watch something. Make sure that there are no distractions that might keep you from what you're supposed to be doing.

Once you manage to kick the habit, you'll notice that you have a lot more free time that you can fill with other things. Your quality of work will improve, and your inner drive, and you'll feel more positive. You'll probably also notice that you reach your goals easier.

Activity Fifty-Four: Completing a Task

Do you know one thing you've been putting off for days or weeks? Now is the time to tackle it.

Identify a task that you know you need to complete but have been putting off. Find a way to break it into smaller pieces and write down these subtasks. Set a timeframe and decide when and how you will complete each one. Once you've completed the task, reflect on the experience and how it felt to overcome the procrastination and get it done!

Whenever you find yourself putting off a task again, think about how good it felt to finally complete this task and use the same approach to get it done.

CHAPTER 7 SUMMARY

- Reframing our minds to see the positive in a situation can make all the difference in how we feel about it.
- When we start our day on a positive note, it sets the tone for the entire day.
- Gratitude is more than just a feeling. Expressing gratitude helps us to focus on the good things we have going for us and flows into positive thinking.
- By having daily routines, we can ensure that we are more focused and efficient every day. Daily routines help us to know what to expect from our day and take the stress of planning away.
- Procrastination steals precious time from us. There are many reasons why we may choose to procrastinate, but it's important not to let it win every time. We need to learn new skills and techniques to help us manage and avoid procrastination.

The next chapter deals with strategies for you to keep your motivation high over the long term and ways in which you can inspire those around you. We'll explore how to avoid burnout and why personal growth is a never-ending journey.

SUSTAINING MOTIVATION AND INSPIRING OTHERS

This chapter is all about keeping that motivation going and inspiring those around you to stay motivated and reach their goals. It's not always easy to keep going, but the main thing to remember is why you started in the first place. Think back to the reason and see the bigger picture.

Don't give up on your goals and dreams. You don't know who might be looking up to you for inspiration and motivation. You might be the reason someone is pursuing something. Keep at it, and don't give up.

To showcase why this is important, let's compare Caroline and Brian.

Caroline has learned how to keep her motivation levels up and chase what she wants from life. Whenever her friends feel a little down and burned out, she shares her energy and motivation with them to keep them going. She is always smiling and pushing forward, and believes anyone can do anything. Her infectious personality is bliss to her friends, and they love being around her.

Brian can't seem to stay motivated, even for the smallest things. He loses focus easily and needs someone like Caroline in his life to keep him going. Unfortunately, because of his overall demeanor and negativity, people like Caroline find it very difficult to be around him. He can't positively influence anyone.

It's difficult being the person no one wants to be around because you're always carrying a dark cloud with you. In this chapter, we'll explore how to keep the motivation going, not burn out in the process, inspire others, and what the journey ahead should look like.

KEEPING THE MOTIVATION FIRE BURNING

We've already discussed how to become motivated, but sometimes, keeping the momentum going is the problem. Apply all of the techniques in this book, such as positive self-talk, mindfulness, having a clear vision, joining a community, creating a routine, and celebrating small wins. You shouldn't have an issue staying motivated. Just in case you need some extra help, here are some additional tips:

- Find someone that you look up to who can mentor you on your journey. Maybe they run a successful business, or they've been through a lot and remain positive. Whatever great qualities they have, learn from them.

- Find some form of exercise for your mental health and to help relieve stress.
- Be around positive people. The more positive they are, the more positive you will be. We really do become the average of the people we spend the most time with. Make sure that those people are good.
- Remember to track your goals throughout and make any adjustments when you feel it's necessary.
- When you reach a goal, set a new one. Don't run out of goals and, therefore, out of things to work toward. Make sure that you always replace your goals once you are successful.

This whole book is about having a motivational mindset. Why is it important? Because it helps us achieve long-term goals and reach success. Success means something different for everyone. With the right motivation, you can succeed regardless of what that looks like.

Activity Fifty-Five: Go Back in Time

Learning from past mistakes is a great way to become a better version of ourselves. This is why we're doing it so often.

Identify a past situation where you worked toward something and then lost motivation. With the knowledge you have now, what do you think you could have done differently to stay motivated? Write it down and reflect on how you will implement those things to ensure it doesn't happen again.

When we consciously decide what we need to change, we allow our brains to plan ahead and know what should happen when faced with a similar situation instead of defaulting to what it normally does.

Activity Fifty-Six: Motivation List

This is not necessarily a list of rewards to motivate you to keep going. It's a list to help keep you motivated.

Grab your pen and paper and list three daily or weekly actions you can take to help keep you motivated. Use the previous section and the earlier chapters to help you with your list. At the end of the week, review your actions and note how they affected your motivation levels. Identify any changes you may need to make.

This activity helps to make the learnings from the book practical to help keep you motivated, even during the toughest times.

HOW TO DODGE BURNOUT

Burnout is a point we can reach where our physical, mental, and emotional states are negatively affected, and we feel too tired and demotivated to do anything. Once we reach that point, it's tough, and it takes a while to get out of it. This can definitely put a big pause on reaching our goals because we lose all motivation.

If you experience any of the following, it might be a sign of burnout:

- no motivation to do anything, even things that are important
- what used to be enjoyable for you now feels like work
- not wanting to eat even your favorite meal
- increased headaches and body pains
- being more irritable than usual and getting upset over almost anything
- always tired, regardless of how much you've slept
- getting sick more often
- not meeting deadlines that should be easy to meet

The moment you start seeing any sign of burnout, act immediately to minimize its effect on your mindset and overall well-being. Here are some things you can do to prevent burnout:

- Spend some time outdoors. Just a bit of Vitamin D from the sun and the fresh air will help to clear your mind and re-energize you to do whatever you need to do.
- Have fun. It's important to always make time to have a little bit of fun. We can't always be working and doing the boring things. Take some time to let your hair down and just relax a bit.
- Make sure that your goals are reasonable and achievable. The SMART goal methodology should help with this, so be sure to use it when setting new goals.
- Be active. Remember to find a physical activity that you enjoy and practice it daily if you can. Stay hydrated by

drinking enough water and follow a balanced diet. A balanced diet does not mean you eat less of everything. It means that you eat enough of every food group based on your body composition and level of activity. See a dietician if you need help with this.

- Get enough sleep. Get into bed at a reasonable hour and ensure that you get between seven and nine hours of sleep every night. You can't catch up on sleep. Once you lose it, it's gone.
- Take sufficient breaks in between tasks. It's impossible to focus on a task for too long fully. You need breaks. It's also not good to be stressed out for a prolonged period of time. Take breaks when you need them, whether it's in between tasks or recharging over a weekend.
- Make time for yourself. Self-care is so important. You need some time to just take care of yourself. Good hygiene, stress relief, and making an effort every day are all great forms of self-care. Make sure that you check in with your mind and body on how they're feeling. Most of the points mentioned above are aspects of self-care.

If you've already reached burnout, it's not too late. Try to get help from a professional as soon as possible. Don't ignore it in the hopes that it will go away. It might just get worse. Manage your stress levels by avoiding anything that will stress you out during the burnout phase and make the necessary changes to prevent it.

Activity Fifty-Seven: A Burnout Journal

Writing things down is the easiest way to remember them. We sometimes forget mental notes, which can lead to missing important signs of burnout.

Keep a journal of any possible signs of stress or fatigue that you might experience for a week. If it's regular and it feels very heavy, take immediate steps to avoid burnout.

By tracking any possible signs, it will be easier to recognize burnout before it's too late. Don't ignore it or brush it off as feeling just a little anxious. Always take possible signs of burnout seriously.

Activity Fifty-Eight: Self-Care Habits

Self-care means to take care of yourself. It sounds easy, but it can be quite difficult when you prioritize everything else in your life, which we tend to do more often than not. We would rather focus on everything and everyone else than our own well-being.

Implement a new self-care habit into your daily routine this week that you either perform only now and then or never at all. After the week, reflect on any changes in your well-being after practicing this new habit. Once it becomes such a normal part of your routine, try to introduce another one.

Taking care of ourselves first should be a priority to avoid burnout. If we reach the burnout stage, we can't do anything for ourselves or others. You can't pour from an empty cup, so make sure that you fill your cup as much as possible.

BE AN INSPIRATION TO OTHERS

One of the best feelings I've experienced is seeing someone I've inspired succeed. It's such a rewarding experience because you know that you've had a hand in it. They did all the work, but you were able to stand on the sidelines and cheer them on. You were part of their success.

Inspiring others is more than just that, though. They won't all become successful. However, when we inspire others, we make their lives better. We show them that they can achieve more than they think, and we make friends in the process. What's even more, you learn a lot about yourself as well. Whatever is inspiring them will showcase your strengths and the skills that you bring to the table.

If you want to be more influential, here are a few tips to get you started.

- **Allow others to share their ideas:** As much as you want to be the inspiration, it's important to allow those around you to freely speak and give their own ideas on what they think would work in a situation. People like being heard.
- **Always keep your word:** If you say you will do something, make sure that you follow through on it. People like having someone that they can depend on.

Someone who never follows through on their promises can't positively influence anyone.

- **Listen more than you speak:** This can sometimes be difficult, but I'm sure you know the old saying: You were given one mouth and two ears so that you can listen twice as much as you speak—or something like that. When someone is talking to you, don't interrupt them. Wait for them to finish speaking before you contribute to the conversation.

- **Show interest:** Get to know the people around you. It's not always just about you speaking to them and teaching them things. You need to learn what they like, what makes them tick, what they're most looking forward to, and what they're working toward. Knowing these things can help you have a bigger influence.

Inspiring others is more than just influencing them. You need to also know how to encourage them to be the best version of themselves, not a copy of you. You can encourage others by speaking life into their situation, letting them know how amazing they are (verbally or written), acknowledging them when they do something great, being there when they need you, and helping them when in need.

Activity Fifty-Nine: Find Someone to Inspire

We all want to inspire others. Why wait for it to happen naturally if you can do it intentionally? It's one of the characteristics of an influential person, to be intentional.

Identify someone in your life that you would like to inspire and plan how you want to do it. Write down your plan and execute it, writing down any observations. Reflect on how it felt to inspire someone else and what you learned from the experience.

We all have something to give to others, so don't be shy about wanting to inspire or influence someone else. There are so many benefits to it, including a confidence boost.

THE ONGOING JOURNEY OF SELF-IMPROVEMENT

Self-improvement is not a once-off thing that you can just quickly do and then move on from. It's a continuous journey throughout our lives. There is always more that we can improve on and get better at. The aim is not to be better than the next person but to be better than the person you were yesterday. Even someone who is a master at something can still improve at it. There is always room for improvement, so never stop working on yourself.

One of the aspects of self-improvement is continuous learning, which incidentally is also a characteristic of an influential person. We need to always be hungry to learn more about whatever strikes our fancy, but also what is relevant in the world today. Staying up to date with current events is a great way to be able to join in on conversations you would have otherwise been excluded from.

If you want to be successful in life, define what success means to you, set goals, and always work toward achieving them. Don't give up. You've got this.

Activity Sixty: Looking to the Future

Let's make one more plan for the future before we move into our 31-day motivational mindset challenge.

Make a list of three skills or habits that you would like to develop for future growth. Using the skills you learned in earlier chapters, create a simple plan to start working on these skills or habits. Reflect on what steps you've taken and how they've started to impact your growth.

Once you've done this, don't be afraid to do it again. And again. You can never improve yourself too much.

CHAPTER 8 SUMMARY

- Some things you can do to keep motivation levels high include finding a mentor, exercising, surrounding yourself with positive people, tracking your goals, and setting new ones.
- It's important to understand what burnout is, how it presents, and how you can avoid it. Never try to do too much at once, and give yourself a break every now and then.
- Inspiring others is a very rewarding thing to do because you know that you're making a difference in their lives.

- We should never stop learning and trying to improve ourselves because there is always more we can do.

The last chapter is a 31-day challenge that provides a practical, day-by-day plan for you to build a stronger motivational mindset in just one month. It serves as a culminating exercise that brings together all the strategies and insights shared in the previous chapters.

31-DAY MOTIVATIONAL MINDSET CHALLENGE

Meet Rica and Gideon: two teens who are at the same school but on completely different paths. Rica starts her month bogged down by stress, unsure of her goals, and lacking motivation. Gideon, however, decides to take up the 31-day motivational mindset challenge. By the end of the month, their lives have diverged in ways neither could have predicted. Are you a Rica, or are you ready to become a Gideon? Take on this 31-day challenge and see for yourself!

31-DAY MOTIVATIONAL CHALLENGE

Day 1: Rise and shine affirmations: Start your day with positive affirmations that set the tone for motivation and success.

Day 2: Dream big, set goals: Visualize your dreams and set achievable goals that align with your passions and aspirations.

Day 3: Gratitude blitz: Write down 10 things you're grateful for and share them with someone who inspires you.

Day 4: Sweat it out: Engage in a physical activity or workout that gets your blood pumping and boosts your energy.

Day 5: Read for inspiration: Dive into a motivational book or article that ignites your drive and expands your horizons.

Day 6: Mindful moments: Practice mindfulness through meditation or deep breathing exercises to enhance focus and clarity.

Day 7: Surround yourself: Spend time with positive and supportive friends or family members who lift you up and encourage your growth.

Day 8: Random acts of kindness: Perform three acts of kindness throughout the day to make a positive impact on others' lives.

Day 9: Explore a new skill: Step out of your comfort zone and learn something new that excites you and broadens your abilities.

Day 10: Reflect and learn: Review your past accomplishments and setbacks, extract valuable lessons, and identify areas for improvement.

Day 11: Visualization power hour: Dedicate an hour to visualizing your goals and success, reinforcing your motivation and determination.

Day 12: Mindset makeover: Identify and challenge negative beliefs or self-doubt, replacing them with empowering thoughts and beliefs.

Day 13: Mentor connection: Seek guidance from a mentor or role model who inspires you and can provide valuable advice and insights.

Day 14: Embrace failure: Embrace the idea that failures are stepping stones to success and view setbacks as opportunities for growth.

Day 15: Creative expression: Engage in a creative activity of your choice, allowing your imagination to flow freely and inspire you. Give examples.

Day 16: Energizing breaks: Take short breaks between tasks to engage in physical activities or relaxation techniques that recharge your energy.

Day 17: Personal development webinars: Look up and book a webinar or workshop on personal growth and self-improvement.

Day 18: Goal mapping: Create a visual map of your goals, breaking them down into actionable steps and timelines.

Day 19: Empathy day: Put yourself in someone else's shoes and practice empathy, seeking to understand and support others.

Day 20: Mindset mantras: Create and repeat personalized affirmations, reinforcing your motivational mindset and boosting confidence.

Day 21: Strength in service: Volunteer your time or skills to a cause that resonates with you, contributing to a greater purpose.

Day 22: Positive people audit: Evaluate the people in your life and consciously surround yourself with positive influences.

Day 23: Mastering time: Optimize your time management skills by prioritizing tasks effectively and minimizing distractions.

Day 24: Problem-solving power: Engage in critical thinking exercises or puzzles that strengthen problem-solving abilities. Give examples.

Day 25: Celebrate milestones: Acknowledge and celebrate your achievements, no matter how small, to stay motivated and inspired.

Day 26: Nature connection: Spend time outdoors, connecting with nature and finding inspiration in its beauty and tranquility.

Day 27: Motivational podcast marathon: Listen to a series of motivational podcasts or TED Talks to expand your knowledge and perspectives.

Day 28: Mindset journaling: Reflect on your thoughts, emotions, and progress through journaling, fostering self-awareness and growth.

Day 29: Harnessing feedback: Seek feedback from trusted individuals and use it constructively to improve and refine your skills.

Day 30: Visualization in action: Take a tangible step toward one of your goals, putting your visualizations into practice.

Day 31: Motivational mastery: Reflect on your transformative journey, embracing your newfound motivational mindset as a foundation for ongoing success.

Once you have completed the 31-day challenge, reflect on how it has changed your life and share your experience with someone else. Encourage them to take on the challenge as well! And remember, you can do this challenge over and over again. In fact, I would encourage you to do it as often as possible. The more you practice how to adopt a motivational mindset, the more your mindset will change.

Congratulations on finishing the book and learning how to cultivate a motivational mindset. The work doesn't stop here, though. It's important that you keep working on it every day, because once you stop focusing on it, your old habits might start coming back. Use the skills, tools, and tips in this book to completely change your life. I promise you that you won't regret it!

CONCLUSION

A motivational mindset will help you reach heights you never thought were possible. You can dream big and know that you will get there. Nothing is out of reach when you know where you are going and what you are capable of. Self-discovery and self-improvement are the two main themes that underpin reaching your full potential.

You don't have to be the best at everything to be successful. You just need to be the best you can be. It all begins with the right mindset. Once you adopt the right mindset, it can be a game-changer in your life.

Some of the things that you need to work on are the skills and ambitions that are unique to you. These will influence your journey and the goals you will set. Understanding your potential and interests is the foundation of future success, which should be accompanied by high self-esteem and resilience.

Remember that a bit of creativity goes a long way when it feels like you're stuck. Turn to some of your interests and passions, or find new hobbies that can inspire you. Another way to boost motivation is to set goals that are SMART in nature and track your progress while rewarding small wins.

Effective time management skills are imperative when we're working toward achieving our goals and leading a balanced life. This will also help to instill new, healthy habits that encourage growth and personal development, which will lead to you inspiring those around you to do the same.

I worked with a young adult recently—we'll call her Hannah— who didn't understand the power of a positive and motivational mindset. She lived the same day over and over and couldn't understand why nothing in her life was changing. As the days went by, she became more depressed and isolated herself from everyone around her because she was convinced that it was their fault.

One of her friends referred her to me, and after our first meeting, I gave her some homework to get her mindset right. In the beginning, she didn't understand why we were doing all these exercises and why they were important, but the more she engaged, the more her mindset started to change.

Hannah is now flourishing in every aspect of her life, and even though she never planned to previously, she enrolled for a degree to further her studies. You can do it, too!

Before I say my goodbyes, I would like to ask you to pay it forward and please leave an honest review on Amazon and help others who might need it get the necessary help.

Keep the fire of motivation burning within you, and never forget that you have the power to shape your destiny. Believe in yourself, dream big, and let your unwavering determination lead you to a life filled with passion, purpose, and endless possibilities. You are the author of your own story, so go forth and write a future that is nothing short of extraordinary. I can't wait to hear about your journey.

All my love!

REFERENCWES

Ackerman, C. E. (2018a, July 9). *What is self-confidence? + 9 proven ways to increase it.* Positive Psychology. https://positivepsychology.com/self-confidence/

Ackerman, C. E. (2018b, November 6). *What is self-worth & how do we build it? (Incl. worksheets).* Positive Psychology. https://positivepsychology.com/self-worth/

Amabile, T. M., & Kramer, S. J. (2011, May). *The power of small wins.* Harvard Business Review. https://hbr.org/2011/05/the-power-of-small-wins

Anderson, J. (n.d.). *Misunderstandings about mindsets.* Mindful by Design. https://mindfulbydesign.com/wp-content/uploads/2016/07/Common-Misunderstandings-about-Mindsets-IG%E2%80%8F.pdf

Banerjee, A. (2023, October 3). *The "motivational mindset."* Reputation Today. https://reputationtoday.in/the-motivational-mindset/

Beresin, E. (2019, December 12). 11 self-care tips for teens and young adults. *Psychology Today.* https://www.psychologytoday.com/intl/blog/inside-out-outside-in/201912/11-self-care-tips-teens-and-young-adults

BetterHelp Editorial Team. (2023, October 25). *Why self-worth matters, and how to improve it.* BetterHelp. https://www.betterhelp.com/advice/self-esteem/why-self-worth-matters-and-how-to-improve-it/

Blouin, M. (2022, April 15). *Research review shows self-esteem has long-term benefits.* UC Davis. https://www.ucdavis.edu/curiosity/news/research-review-shows-self-esteem-has-long-term-benefits

Borge, J. (2023, July 25). *40 positive affirmations to add to your daily rotation.* Oprah Daily. https://www.oprahdaily.com/life/relationships-love/g25629970/positive-affirmations/

Brown, E. (2019, February 17). *A universal truth of life: Failure.* Medium. https://medium.com/swlh/a-universal-truth-of-life-failure-981976221e7c

Byrne, D. (2022, June 13). *8 tips on how you can encourage others.* Deborah Byrne Psychology Services. https://deborahbyrnepsychologyservices.com/8-tips-on-how-you-can-encourage-others/

Campbell, S. (2017, March 2). *The 8 magical benefits of resilience.* Entrepreneur. https://www.entrepreneur.com/leadership/the-8-magical-benefits-of-resilience/289923

Carson, J. (n.d.). *Why is creativity important and what does it contribute?* National Youth Council of Ireland. https://www.youth.ie/articles/why-is-creativity-important-and-what-does-it-contribute/

Carter, N. (2021, March 17). 17 ways to find inspiration and spark creativity. *Skillshare Blog.* https://www.skillshare.com/en/blog/17-ways-to-find-inspiration-and-spark-creativity/

Cartwright, D. (2021, December 3). 5 simple steps to leverage your strengths. *The Daily Shifts.* https://www.thedailyshifts.com/blog/5-simple-steps-to-leverage-your-strengths

Cherry, K. (2021, October 29). *What is gratitude?* Verywell Mind. https://www.verywellmind.com/what-is-gratitude-5206817

Cherry, K. (2022, May 23). *Intrinsic motivation vs. extrinsic motivation: What's the difference?* Verywell Mind. https://www.verywellmind.com/differences-between-extrinsic-and-intrinsic-motivation-2795384

Cherry, K. (2023a, May 3). *Motivation: The driving force behind our actions.* Verywell Mind. https://www.verywellmind.com/what-is-motivation-2795378

Cherry, K. (2023b, May 4). *The power of positive thinking.* Verywell Mind. https://www.verywellmind.com/what-is-positive-thinking-2794772

Cherry, K. (2023c, November 13). *What is the negativity bias?* Verywell Mind. https://www.verywellmind.com/negative-bias-4589618

Clarabut, J. (2023, November 19). *The importance of an engaging community.* Wellbeing People. https://www.wellbeingpeople.com/2020/07/23/the-importance-of-an-engaging-community/

Cooks-Campbell, A. (2022, July 11). The importance of knowing yourself: Your key to fulfillment. *BetterUp.* https://www.betterup.com/blog/the-importance-of-knowing-yourself

Cooper, N. (2021, December 1). Why hobbies are important. *NCC Home Learning.* https://www.ncchomelearning.co.uk/blog/importance-of-hobbies/

Daskal, L. (2016, June 22). *19 highly effective ways to stay motivated.* Inc.Africa. https://www.incafrica.com/library/lolly-daskal-19-simple-ways-to-stay-motivated-that-actually-work

Davis, T. (2020, December 3). *What is positive thinking? +9 examples of positive thoughts.* Positive Psychology. https://positivepsychology.com/positive-thinking/

Delaney. (2023, June 13). *100 life accomplishments you should be proud of.* Authentically Del. https://authenticallydel.com/100-life-accomplishments-you-should-be-proud-of/

Dior, C. (2015, October 23). *10 amazing things happen when you inspire others with your experience*. Lifehack. https://www.lifehack.org/323951/10-amazing-things-happen-when-you-inspire-others-with-your-experience

Dube, R. (2021, May 31). Finding your personal vision in 3 easy steps. *Small Giants Community*. https://blog.smallgiants.org/finding-your-personal-vision-in-3-easy-steps

Dyer, D. (n.d.). The benefits & power of celebrating small wins. *Time Well Scheduled*. https://timewellscheduled.com/the-benefits-power-of-celebrating-small-wins/

Earley, B. (2021, March 24). *Here's how to make a vision board for manifestation*. Oprah Daily. https://www.oprahdaily.com/life/a29959841/how-to-make-a-vision-board/

Eatough, E. (2022, August 5). A guide for using motivation to achieve goals. *BetterUp*. https://www.betterup.com/blog/how-motivation-helps-in-achieving-goals

8 self-care tips for teens. (2021, September 21). *Michigan Psychological Care*. https://michiganpsychologicalcare.com/blog/self-care-for-teens.php

18 reasons why a daily routine is so important. (2016, May 27). Skilled at Life. https://www.skilledatlife.com/18-reasons-why-a-daily-routine-is-so-important/

Exercise and mental health. (n.d.). Better Health Channel. https://www.betterhealth.vic.gov.au/health/healthyliving/exercise-and-mental-health

Exercise and mental health. (2023, March). Healthdirect. https://www.healthdirect.gov.au/exercise-and-mental-health

Exercise and teenagers. (n.d.). University of Rochester Medical Center. https://www.urmc.rochester.edu/encyclopedia/content.aspx?ContentTypeID=90&ContentID=P01602

5 ways exercise boosts self-confidence. (2023, September 8). Jazzercise. https://www.jazzercise.com/Community/Blog/5-Ways-Exercise-Boosts-Self-Confidence

5 ways to find what your strengths are. (n.d.). Barclays. https://barclayslifeskills.com/i-want-to-choose-my-next-step/school/5-ways-to-find-out-what-you-re-good-at/

5 ways to prevent high school burnout. (2020, January 24). Parenting Teens and

Tweens. https://parentingteensandtweens.com/5-ways-to-prevent-high-school-burnout/

Forgeard, V. (2022, July 6). *Why is inspiring others important.* Brilliantio. https://brilliantio.com/why-is-inspiring-others-important/

4 reasons why it's important to track your goals and milestones. (n.d.). Nucleus. https://nucleusapp.io/productivity-articles/why-its-important-to-track-your-goals-and-milestones/

Gotter, A. (2020, June 17). *Box breathing.* Healthline. https://www.healthline.com/health/box-breathing

Greene, J. (2023, October 2). How to prioritize tasks when everything feels important. *Zapier.* https://zapier.com/blog/how-to-prioritize/

Guest Author. (2021, August 31). Find your creativity and freedom with a passion project. *DeskTime.* https://desktime.com/blog/passion-project

Hashmi, M. (2022, December 24). *Goal setting theory of motivation.* Quidlo. https://www.quidlo.com/blog/goal-setting-theory-of-motivation/

Healthwise Staff. (2022, October 20). *Learning about thought reframing.* MyHealth.Alberta.ca. https://myhealth.alberta.ca/Health/aftercareinformation/pages/conditions.aspx?hwid=abk7438

Henley, D. (2022, May 22). *Three strategies to help reframe failure.* Forbes. https://www.forbes.com/sites/dedehenley/2022/05/22/three-strategies-to-help-reframe-failure/?sh=7b03f0695b48

Herrity, J. (2023a, July 10). *How to write SMART goals in 5 steps (with examples).* Indeed. https://www.indeed.com/career-advice/career-development/how-to-write-smart-goals

Herrity, J. (2023b, July 31). *How to write an action plan (with template and example).* Indeed. https://www.indeed.com/career-advice/career-development/how-to-write-an-action-plan

Hogarty, S. (2022, August 18). *What is inspiration and why is it so important?* WeWork Ideas. https://www.wework.com/ideas/professional-development/creativity-culture/what-is-inspiration-and-why-is-it-so-important

Hoshaw, C. (2022, June 22). *32 mindfulness activities to find calm at any age.* Healthline. https://www.healthline.com/health/mind-body/mindfulness-activities

Hosie, R. (2018, July 5). How your motivations in life change as you get older, according to new study. *The Independent.* https://www.independent.co.uk/life-style/motivations-life-how-change-older-money-family-yougov-study-a8432521.html

How can you frame and reframe your failures as learning opportunities? (n.d.). LinkedIn. https://www.linkedin.com/advice/1/how-can-you-frame-reframe-your-failures-learning

How to set your personal vision and purpose. (n.d.). *Values Driven Achievement.* https://www.valuesdrivenachievement.com/blog/how-to-set-your-personal-vision-and-purpose

How to track your goals: 10 easiest goal tracking methods. (2020, August 12). Kath Kyle. https://www.kathkyle.com/how-to-track-your-goals/

The importance of a school/life balance. (2022, April 11). Healthy Young NV. https://healthyyoungnv.org/the-importance-of-a-school-life-balance/

Indeed Editorial Team. (2023a, February 4). *14 time-management techniques to improve productivity.* Indeed. https://www.indeed.com/career-advice/career-development/time-management-techniques

Indeed Editorial Team. (2023b, February 4). *What is the Eisenhower matrix? Definition, tasks and tips.* Indeed. https://www.indeed.com/career-advice/career-development/eisenhower-matrix

Island Futures Skills & Participation. (2020). Skills, qualities and duties - what's the difference? In *Isle of Wight Council.* https://www.iow.gov.uk/azservices/documents/1696-Skills-qualities-duties-handout.pdf

Jenkins, P. (2022a, May 3). *Why is motivation important (explained with examples).* Brilliantio. https://brilliantio.com/why-is-motivation-important/

Jenkins, P. (2022b, September 13). *Why Creativity is Important.* Brilliantio. https://brilliantio.com/why-creativity-is-important/

Kaiser, E. (2023, June 6). What is self-awareness and why is it important. *Better Kids.* https://betterkids.education/blog/what-is-self-awareness-and-why-is-it-important

Legere, C. (2020, September 24). *What's the difference between self-esteem and self-confidence?* Toronto Psychologists. https://www.torontopsychologists.com/whats-the-difference-between-self-esteem-and-self-confidence

Logan, T. (n.d.). Why having a vision is the most important aspect of your life. *Conscious Magazine.* https://consciousmagazine.co/why-having-a-vision-is-the-most-important-aspect-of-your-life/

Macmillan, R. (2021, August 19). How to make time for your hobbies–and why you should! *Freedom Matters.* https://freedom.to/blog/make-time-for-your-hobbies/

Makvana, H. (2023, November 14). *69 fun teenage hobbies to choose from.* Mom

Junction. https://www.momjunction.com/articles/teenagers-hobbies_00474362/

Malec, M. (2022, February 7). *Continuous learning: What it is, why it's important, and how to support it.* Learnerbly. https://www.learnerbly.com/articles/continuous-learning-what-it-is-why-its-important-and-how-to-support-it

Mathias, R. J. (n.d.). *What is a motivated mindset?* Mathias Method. https://mathiasmethod.com/what-is-a-motivated-mindset/

Mayo Clinic Staff. (2022, July 14). *Resilience: Build skills to endure hardship.* Mayo Clinic. https://www.mayoclinic.org/tests-procedures/resilience-training/in-depth/resilience/art-20046311

Melegrito, R. (2023, June 16). *5 online strengths tests you can take to identify your strengths.* Make Use Of. https://www.makeuseof.com/online-strength-tests-identify-skills/

Melkonian, L. (2021, January 13). The secret behind how to influence people. *BetterUp.* https://www.betterup.com/blog/the-secret-behind-how-to-influence-people

Millacci, T. S. (2017, February 28). *What is gratitude and why is it so important?* Positive Psychology. https://positivepsychology.com/gratitude-appreciation/

Miller, K. (2020, January 30). *5+ ways to develop a growth mindset using grit & resilience.* Positive Psychology. https://positivepsychology.com/5-ways-develop-grit-resilience/

The Mind Tools Content Team. (n.d.-a). *Prioritization.* Mind Tools. https://www.mindtools.com/adwtc03/prioritization

The Mind Tools Content Team. (n.d.-b). *SMART goals.* Mind Tools. https://www.mindtools.com/a4wo118/smart-goals

The Mind Tools Content Team. (n.d.-c). *Using affirmations.* MindTools. https://www.mindtools.com/air49f4/using-affirmations

The Mind Tools Content Team. (n.d.-d). *What is time management?* Mind Tools. https://www.mindtools.com/arb6j5a/what-is-time-management

Moore, C. (2019, December 30). *What is the negativity bias and how can it be overcome?* Positive Psychology. https://positivepsychology.com/3-steps-negativity-bias/#overcome

Moore, L. (2015, August 18). 8 ways to provide power of encouragement. *Democrat and Chronicle.* https://www.democratandchronicle.com/story/news/health/2015/08/18/eight-ways-provide-power-encouragement/31905023/

Motivation myth buster series. (n.d.). American Psychological Association. https:// www.apa.org/ed/schools/myth-busters

Motivation: How to get started and staying motivated. (2022, July). Healthdirect Australia. https://www.healthdirect.gov.au/motivation-how-to-get-started-and-staying-motivated

9 proven time management techniques and tools | USAHS. (2019, October 3). *University of St. Augustine for Health Sciences.* https://www.usa.edu/blog/time-management-techniques/

OConnell, E. (2019, March 14). *Failure is the universal experience that binds us all. So why shouldn't we express it?* Image. https://www.image.ie/editorial/the-importance-of-failure-124297

Odendahl, S. (2023). *Youth activity: Manage your time for well-being.* University of Minnesota Extension. https://extension.umn.edu/youth-learning-and-skills/daily-time-management-wellbeing

Parsons, L. (2022, October 14). 8 time management tips for students. *Harvard Summer School.* https://summer.harvard.edu/blog/8-time-management-tips-for-students/

Peale, N. V. (n.d.). *Norman Vincent Peale* quotes. Goodreads. https://www. goodreads.com/quotes/4324-shoot-for-the-moon-even-if-you-miss-you-ll-land

Perry, E. (2022a, March 3). 30 positive affirmations to add to your mental strength workout. *BetterUp.* https://www.betterup.com/blog/positive-affir mations

Perry, E. (2022b, March 30). Self-esteem isn't everything, but these 5 tips can give you a boost. *BetterUp.* https://www.betterup.com/blog/how-to-improve-self-esteem

Perry, E. (2022c, May 18). Learn how to be your own best ally for reaching your goals. *BetterUp.* https://www.betterup.com/blog/what-is-self-motivation

Perry, E. (2022d, September 14). What is self-awareness and how to develop it. *BetterUp.* https://www.betterup.com/blog/what-is-self-awareness

Perry, E. (2023, June 15). What are vision boards & how to create one for manifestation. *BetterUp.* https://www.betterup.com/blog/how-to-create-vision-board

Poirot, K. (n.d.). *Ken Poirot quotes.* Goodreads. https://www.goodreads.com/quotes/9894362-today-is-your-opportunity-to-build-the-tomorrow-you-want

Positive self-talk. (2021). In *The Counseling and Wellness Center.* Western Washington University. https://cwc.wwu.edu/files/2021-09/wwu_positive_ self_talk_worksheet.pdf

Price, A. (2018, April 17). 4 reasons why teens can't stop procrastinating. *Psychology Today.* https://www.psychologytoday.com/us/blog/the-unmoti vated-teen/201804/4-reasons-why-teens-cant-stop-procrastinating

Prioritization. (n.d.). Product Plan. https://www.productplan.com/glossary/ prioritization/

Psychology Today Staff. (n.d.). *Motivation.* Psychology Today. https://www. psychologytoday.com/us/basics/motivation

Raeburn, A. (2023, January 8). *Create an action plan that drives results.* Asana. https://asana.com/resources/action-plan

Reed, P. (2021, December 15). *Physical activity is good for the mind and the body.* U.S. Department of Health and Human Services. https://health.gov/news/ 202112/physical-activity-good-mind-and-body

Ritter, C. (2023, May 2). *New survey finds teens happier, more motivated.* EdChoice. https://www.edchoice.org/engage/new-survey-finds-teens-happier-more-motivated/

Robert. (2023, May 26). *Time management for teens: Tips for parents.* Time Hack Hero. https://timehackhero.com/time-management-for-teens-tips-for-parents/

Ross. (n.d.). *How to break down goals into steps.* The Disciplined Rebel. https:// disciplinedrebel.com/how-to-break-down-goals-into-steps/

Roosevelt, T. (n.d.). *Theodore Roosevelt quotes.* BrainyQuote. https://www. brainyquote.com/quotes/theodore_roosevelt_380703

Rosser, J. (2022, May 4). *17 benefits of high self-esteem. What is it and do you have it?* Success Stream. https://www.success-stream.co.uk/17-benefits-high-self-esteem/

Saraev, N. (2022, May 19). The top 10 most common time wasters & how to avoid them. *Day.io.* https://day.io/blog/the-top-10-most-common-time-wasters-how-to-avoid-them/

Savage, C. (n.d.). *Negative bias | learning how to overcome negative thinking.* The Better You Institute. https://thebetteryouinstitute.com/2022/04/20/nega tive-bias-overcome-negative-thinking/

Schuldt, B. (n.d.). *The importance of setting goals and tracking progress for better decision making.* Tability. https://www.tability.io/odt-articles/the-importance-of-setting-goals-and-tracking-progress-for-better-decision-making

Self-esteem and self-confidence. (2019, October 29). The University of Queensland. https://my.uq.edu.au/information-and-services/student-support/health-and-wellbeing/self-help-resources/self-esteem-and-self-confidence

Self-Talk definition: 6 ways to practice positive self-talk daily. (2022, July 15). MasterClass. https://www.masterclass.com/articles/self-talk

Seven reasons why continuous learning is important. (n.d.). Education Executive. https://edexec.co.uk/seven-reasons-why-continuous-learning-is-important/

7 ways how to identify your personal strengths. (n.d.). High 5 Test. https://high5test.com/identifying-personal-strengths/

Smith, R., & Harte, V. (2021, June 28). *How to write your own affirmations.* Dummies. https://www.dummies.com/article/body-mind-spirit/emotional-health-psychology/emotional-health/general-emotional-health/how-to-write-your-own-affirmations-145446/

Souders, B. (2019a, November 5). *20 most popular theories of motivation in psychology.* Positive Psychology. https://positivepsychology.com/motivation-theories-psychology/

Souders, B. (2019b, November 5). *Motivation and what really drives human behavior.* Positive Psychology. https://positivepsychology.com/motivation-human-behavior/

Souders, B. (2019c, November 5). *What is motivation? A psychologist explains.* Positive Psychology. https://positivepsychology.com/what-is-motivation/

Straw, E. (2023, November 21). Importance of goal setting. *Success Starts Within.* https://www.successstartswithin.com/blog/importance-of-goal-setting

Team FF. (2021, November 1). *5 ways fitness can help your self-confidence.* Fitness First. https://www.fitnessfirst.com.my/blog/5-ways-fitness-can-help-your-self-confidence

10 best prioritization techniques in 2023. (2023, December 15). *Timeular.* https://timeular.com/blog/best-prioritization-techniques/

10 major benefits of self motivation for a progressive life. (n.d.). Sanjeev Datta Personality School. https://sanjeevdatta.com/benefits-of-self-motivation/

10 passion project ideas for high school students. (2023, March 30). Crimson Education. https://www.crimsoneducation.org/nz/blog/passion-project-ideas/

10 reasons why creativity is important. (2023, January 1). *Yonobi.* https://yonobi.com/blogs/news/being-creative-and-why-its-important-for-our-well-being

10 tips for improving your self-esteem. (n.d.). Reachout. https://au.reachout.com/articles/10-tips-for-improving-your-self-esteem

10 traits of highly motivated people. (2022, February 24). *Agile Meridian*. https://www.agilemeridian.com/blog/10-traits-of-highly-motivated-people

10 ways stopping procrastination benefits you. (2022, September 18). Positivity Guides. https://www.positivityguides.net/10-ways-stopping-procrastination-benefits-you/

10 ways to spark creative thinking. (n.d.). Virtues for Life. https://www.virtuesforlife.com/10-ways-to-spark-creative-thinking/

Top 50 hobbies for teens (that aren't sports, computers, or gaming). (2019, January 2). *Evolve Treatment Centers.* https://evolvetreatment.com/blog/hobbies-teens/

Torgerson, D. (2023, May 19). 10 passion project ideas for high school students. *Alludo.* https://blog.alludolearning.com/10-passion-project-ideas-for-high-school-students

Toso, C. (2023, May 18). *How to find and join a community of practice.* Commsor. https://www.commsor.com/post/a-beginners-guide-to-joining-community-of-practice

Understand yourself and know your potential. (2013, November 15). Morgan McKinley. https://www.morganmckinley.com.cn/en/article/understand-yourself-and-know-your-potential

Vemparala, T. (2023, November 8). *Track your goals with these 10 free tools.* Business News Daily. https://www.businessnewsdaily.com/10495-track-goals-tools.html

Waehner, P. (2022, February 12). *What a complete workout schedule looks like.* Verywell Fit. https://www.verywellfit.com/sample-workout-schedule-1230758

What is academic burnout? (2019, November 13). *University of the People.* https://www.uopeople.edu/blog/what-is-academic-burnout/

What is gratitude. (2019). Greater Good. https://greatergood.berkeley.edu/topic/gratitude/definition

What is vision and why is having vision important? (n.d.). *University of the People.* https://www.uopeople.edu/blog/what-is-vision-and-its-importance/

Where do you find the best online and offline communities for your field? (n.d.). LinkedIn. https://www.linkedin.com/advice/3/where-do-you-find-best-online-offline-communities

Whipps, K. (2021, December 20). 20 brilliant ways to track your goals. *Brush Up.* https://creativemarket.com/blog/ways-to-track-your-goals

Whitener, S. (2019, February 7). *The lifelong journey of personal development.* Forbes. https://www.forbes.com/sites/forbescoachescouncil/2019/02/07/the-lifelong-journey-of-personal-development/?sh=7be3fb5c2596

Why you put things off until the last minute. (2022, December 4). McLean Hospital. https://www.mcleanhospital.org/essential/procrastination

Wong, S. J. (2021, August 5). *13 things that don't determine your self-worth.* Shine. https://advice.theshineapp.com/articles/12-things-that-dont-determine-your-self-worth/

Wooll, M. (2021, November 3). Community for the win - how collective solutions help individual problems. *BetterUp.* https://www.betterup.com/blog/importance-of-community

Wrighton, F. (2019, July 1). *23 ways to spark your creativity.* Jenny Garrett Global. https://jennygarrett.global/23-ways-to-spark-your-creativity/

Wu, R. (2022, October 10). 6 reasons why having a hobby is important. *Maniology.* https://maniology.com/blogs/maniology-blog/why-are-hobbies-important

Young, A. (2021, April 26). 7 common obstacles to your goals and how to navigate them. *Rainmakers.* https://gorainmakers.com/2021/04/26/7-common-obstacles-to-your-goals-and-how-to-navigate-them/

Made in the USA
Las Vegas, NV
12 October 2024

96749328R00089